....................................................

To:

....................................................

From:

....................................................

Date:

# Jesus Calling®
## ~for~
# Graduates

*Sarah Young*

THOMAS NELSON
*Since 1798*

Jesus Calling® for Graduates

© 2016 Sarah Young
Devotions are previously published from *Jesus Calling* © 2004

Published in Nashville, Tennessee, by Thomas Nelson. Thomas Nelson is a registered trademark of HarperCollins Christian Publishing.

Thomas Nelson titles may be purchased in bulk for educational, business, fund-raising, or sales promotional use. For information, please e-mail SpecialMarkets@ ThomasNelson.com.

Unless otherwise noted, Scripture quotations are taken from the Holy Bible, New International Version®, NIV®. Copyright © 1973, 1978, 1984 by Biblica, Inc.™ Used by permission of Zondervan. All rights reserved worldwide. www.zondervan.com

Other Scripture quotations are from the following sources:

The King James Version (KJV). *The Message* (MSG). Copyright © 1993, 1994, 1995, 1996, 2000, 2001, 2002. Used by permission of Tyndale House Publishers, Inc. The New King James Version® (NKJV). Copyright © 1982 by Thomas Nelson. Used by permission. All rights reserved. The New American Standard Bible® (NASB), Copyright © 1960, 1962, 1963, 1968, 1971, 1972, 1973, 1975, 1977, 1995 by The Lockman Foundation. Used by permission. The Amplified Bible (AMP), Copyright © 1954, 1958, 1962, 1964, 1965, 1987 by The Lockman Foundation, La Habra, CA. All rights reserved. Used by permission. www.lockman.org.

ISBN: 978-0-7180-9938-1 (custom)

Printed in China

21 22 23 DSC 8 7 6

# Contents

## RENEWING YOUR MIND

## TIME

## TRUST

## WEAKNESS

## WORTH

Dear Graduate,

Congratulations on your accomplishment! I hope you are able to savor this moment in your life—this moment in time that is full of celebration and anticipation of new beginnings.

You might be moving away for the first time, going to college, starting a new job, or perhaps doing all three. Whatever journey you find yourself about to embark on, I would like to share some truths I have carried with me on my own journeys.

No matter what season of life we find ourselves in, we can rest in the knowledge that Jesus is our constant. When changes swirl around us, we can trust that He is the light that shows us the way and the love that never lets us go. Hebrews 13:8 reminds us that Jesus Christ is the same yesterday, today, and forever. What a wonderful encouragement to know that our Savior never changes!

I have found that the more connected I am to Jesus, the more peaceful and content I can be. As you are meeting new people, rising to new challenges, and making many decisions on your own, you need more than ever to stay connected to Him. I hope that this book will remind you Whom to seek when you need guidance, Whom to cling to when you need hope, and Whose presence is with you continually.

Stay faithful in prayer and grounded in biblical truth. May the Lord bless you and keep you close to Him as you set out on the adventure before you.

Beautiful blessings!

*Sarah Young*

# Introduction

## Jesus Calling

I FIRST EXPERIENCED THE PRESENCE OF GOD in a setting of exquisite beauty. I was studying at a Christian community in a tiny Alpine village in France. This was a branch of L'Abri, an international ministry that began in Switzerland through Francis and Edith Schaeffer's work. During my stay at L'Abri, I often explored the fairyland-like environment all around me. It was late winter, and the noonday sun was warm enough for sunbathing, but the depth of the snow kept it from melting. Brilliant sunlight reflecting from pure white snow was cleansing my mind of the darkness that had held it captive for years.

Every day I climbed up a steep hill to attain a view that delighted my soul. As I stood at the top, I would lose myself in a panorama of unbroken beauty. Below me was the village that had become my home. Viewed from this height, the village was dominated by a high-steepled church. Turning 180 degrees, I could see Lake Geneva far below me, shouting greetings in refracted sunbeams. When I looked up, I saw icy tips of Alpine mountains encircling me. I would turn round and round, absorbing as much as I could with two eyes and a finite mind.

The daughter of a college professor, I had been encouraged to read widely and think for myself. I had majored in philosophy at

Wellesley College and had almost completed my master's degree in child development at Tufts University. A few months earlier, my brother had asked me to read Francis Schaeffer's *Escape from Reason*. To my great surprise and delight, that small book had answered questions I'd long before dismissed as unanswerable. It was the intellectual integrity of Schaeffer's books that had drawn me to this pristine place. I was searching for absolute, unchanging truth—a foundation on which to build my life.

Shortly after I settled into the home I shared with other students, I met a gifted counselor who had come from the Swiss branch of L'Abri to talk with some of us. I went into the room where she was waiting, and she told me to close the door. Before I even had time to sit down, she asked her first question: "Are you a Christian?" I answered that I wasn't sure; I wanted to be a Christian, but I didn't really understand why I needed Jesus. I thought that knowing God might be enough. Her second question was: "What can you not forgive yourself for?" This question brought me face to face with my sinfulness, and immediately I understood my need for Jesus—to save me from my many sins. Later, when I was alone, I asked Him to forgive all my sins and to be my Savior-God.

One night I found myself leaving the warmth of our cozy chalet to walk alone in the snowy mountains. I went into a deeply wooded area, feeling vulnerable and awed by cold, moonlit beauty. The air was crisp and dry, piercing to inhale. After a while, I came into an open area and I stopped walking. Time seemed to stand still as I gazed around me in wonder—soaking in the beauty of this place. Suddenly I became aware of a lovely Presence with me, and my involuntary response was to whisper, "Sweet Jesus." This experience of Jesus' Presence was far more personal than the intellectual answers for which I'd been searching. This was a relationship with the Creator of the universe—the One who is *the way, the truth, and the life* (John 14:6 NKJV).

The following year, back in the United States, I had another encounter with the Presence of Jesus. I was grieving the loss of a serious dating relationship and wondering whether being a Christian made much difference in the quality of my life.

At that time I was working as a technical writer in Virginia. My boss sent me to Atlanta to attend a conference. I accepted this assignment dutifully and checked into the hotel without enthusiasm. Alone in my room, I felt waves of desolation wash over me. So I began walking the streets of Atlanta aimlessly, trying to escape my solitude. I glanced at some books in an outdoor stall and was drawn to *Beyond Ourselves* by Catherine Marshall. That night, as I read the book, I no longer felt alone. I knelt beside the bed in that sterile room and felt an overwhelming Presence of peace and love come over me. I knew that Jesus was with me and that He sympathized with my heartache. This was unquestionably the same "Sweet Jesus" I had encountered in the snowy splendor of the Alps.

During the next sixteen years, I lived what many people might consider an exemplary Christian life. I went to Covenant

Theological Seminary in St. Louis, where I earned a master's degree in counseling and biblical studies. While there, I met my husband, Steve, a third-generation missionary to Japan. After graduation, we spent two four-year terms in Japan doing church-planting ministry. We had a baby girl during our first term and a baby boy during our furlough in the United States. After our second term, we returned to the US for three years. We lived in Atlanta, where Steve worked with a local Japanese church and I earned a further degree in counseling at Georgia State University.

As part of my training, I worked at a Christian counseling center in the Atlanta area. I cherished my experiences of helping deeply wounded women find healing in Christ. I was also thankful for my kind, loving husband and our two delightful children, who were the main joys of my life. However, not once during those sixteen years did I vividly experience the Presence of Jesus.

So I was ready to begin a new spiritual quest. It started with delving into a devotional book, *The Secret of the Abiding Presence* by Andrew Murray. The theme of this book is that God's Presence is meant to be the continual experience of Christians. Murray emphasizes the importance of spending time alone with God in quiet, uninterrupted communion.

I began reading the book at a very unstructured time in my life. We were waiting for our Australian visas to be approved so that we could begin a church among Japanese people living in Melbourne. I had quit my counseling job to prepare for the move overseas, so I was adjusting to the loss of this fulfilling work. In the midst of those momentous changes, I began seeking God's Presence in earnest. My days started alone with God, equipped with Bible, devotional book, prayer journal, pen, and coffee. An hour or two alone with Him seemed too brief.

The uncertainties I faced at that time deepened my increasing closeness to God. My husband and I had no idea how long it would take to receive permanent residency visas, so the waiting period seemed to stretch indefinitely into the future. During that period, I had four surgeries, including two for melanoma. A Bible verse that comforted me during this difficult time of waiting also accompanied me on the seemingly endless flight to Australia: "You will go out in joy and be led forth in peace" (Isaiah 55:12).

We settled in Australia and began our dual ministries. I supported Steve in planting the first-ever Japanese church in Melbourne, but my main ministry focus was counseling Australian women, some of whom were coming out of terrible abuse and spiritual bondage.

Our combined ministries subjected our family to intense spiritual warfare, and I prayed for protection every morning. One morning as I prayed, I visualized God protecting each of us. I pictured first our daughter, then our son, and then Steve encircled by God's protective Presence. When I prayed for myself, I was suddenly enveloped in brilliant light and profound peace. I had not sought this powerful experience of God's Presence, but I received it gratefully and was strengthened by it.

Only two or three days later, a counseling client who was an incest survivor began remembering experiences of satanic ritual abuse. This form of Satan worship involves subjecting victims (who are often young children) to incredibly evil, degrading tortures. My courageous client and I walked together into the darkness of her memories. But God had prepared me for stepping into deep darkness by first bathing me in His glorious light. I realized that experiences of God's Presence were not only for my benefit but were also preparation for helping others.

The following year, I began to wonder if I could change my prayer times from monologue to dialogue. I had been writing in prayer journals for many years, but this was one-way communication: I did all the talking. Increasingly, I wanted to hear what God might want to communicate to me on a given day. I decided to "listen" with pen in hand, writing down whatever I "heard" in my mind. As J. I. Packer wrote in his book *Your Father Loves You*: "God . . . guides our minds as we think things out in his presence." This is how I was listening to Him—by focusing on Jesus and His Word, while asking Him to guide my thoughts. I was not listening for an audible voice; I was spending time *seeking God's Face* (Psalm 27:8 NKJV).

My journaling thus changed from monologue to dialogue. This new way of communicating with God became the high point of my day. Of course, I knew my writings were not inspired—as only Scripture is—but they were helping me grow closer to God. This became a delightful way to *encourage myself in the Lord* (1 Samuel 30:6 KJV).

As I was learning to seek God's Face, "Be still, and know that I am God" (Psalm 46:10) became a life-changing verse. Alternate readings for "Be still" are "Relax," "Let go," and "Cease striving" (NASB). This is an enticing invitation from God to lay down our cares and seek His Presence.

Among other resources, *Praying: Finding Our Way Through Duty to Delight* has been helpful. This book, written by J. I. Packer, and Carolyn Nystrom, contains a wonderful quote from Martin Luther—"If the Holy Spirit should come and begin to preach to your heart, giving you rich and enlightened thoughts, . . . be quiet and listen to him who can talk better than you; and note what he proclaims and *write it down*; so will you experience miracles as David says: 'Open my eyes that I may behold wondrous things out of thy law' (Psalm 119:18)."

During the years that I've been waiting in God's Presence and listening with pen in hand, I have found themes of His Peace becoming more prominent in my writing. I'm sure this tendency reflects, in part, my personal need. However, when people open up to me, I find that most of them also desire the balm of Jesus' Peace.

This practice of being still in God's Presence has increased my intimacy with Him more than any other spiritual discipline, so I want to share some of the writings I have gleaned from these quiet moments. In many parts of the world, Christians seem to be searching for a deeper experience of Jesus' Presence and Peace. The devotions that follow address that felt need.

The Bible is the only infallible, inerrant Word of God, and I endeavor to keep my writings consistent with that unchanging standard. I have written from the perspective of Jesus speaking, to help readers feel more personally connected with Him. So the first person singular ("I," "Me," "My," "Mine") always refers to Christ; "you" refers to you, the reader.

I have included Scripture references after each daily reading. As I waited in God's Presence, Bible verses or fragments of verses often came to mind. So I interwove these into the devotions. Words from the Scriptures (some paraphrased, some quoted) are indicated in italics. Certain Bible verses figure rather heavily in my writing. That is because God often uses these passages to strengthen and encourage me, raising my sights from my "light and momentary troubles" (2 Corinthians 4:17) to His eternal perspective.

Themes of thankfulness and trust recurred often during my listening times. These themes are quite prevalent in the Bible, and they are essential for a close relationship with the Lord.

The devotions in this book are meant to be read slowly, preferably in a quiet place—with your Bible open. Remember that Jesus is Immanuel, *God with us*. May you enjoy His Presence and His Peace in ever-increasing measure.

*Sarah Young*

# Adversity

# Overcoming Obstacles

I AM WITH YOU AND FOR YOU. When you decide on a course of action that is in line with My will, nothing in heaven or on earth can stop you. You may encounter many obstacles as you move toward your goal, but don't be discouraged—never give up! With My help, you can overcome any obstacle. Do not expect an easy path as you journey hand in hand with Me, but do remember that I, your *very-present Helper*, am omnipotent.

Much, much stress results from your wanting to make things happen before their times have come. One of the main ways I assert My sovereignty is in the timing of events. If you want to stay close to Me and do things My way, ask Me to show you the path forward moment by moment. Instead of dashing headlong toward your goal, let Me set the pace. Slow down, and enjoy the journey in My Presence.

*What, then, shall we say in response to this? If*
*God is for us, who can be against us?*

ROMANS 8:31

*Also read:*

PSALM 46:1–3 NKJV; LUKE 1:37

I AM LEADING YOU ALONG THE HIGH ROAD, but there are descents as well as ascents. In the distance you see snow-covered peaks glistening in brilliant sunlight. Your longing to reach those peaks is good, but you must not take shortcuts. Your assignment is to follow Me, allowing Me to direct your path. Let the heights beckon you onward, but stay close to Me.

Learn to trust Me when things go "wrong." Disruptions to your routine highlight your dependence on Me. Trusting acceptance of trials brings blessings that *far outweigh them all*. Walk hand in hand with Me through this day. I have lovingly planned every inch of the way. Trust does not falter when the path becomes rocky and steep. Breathe deep draughts of My Presence, and hold tightly to My hand. Together we can make it!

*Jesus said this to indicate the kind of death by which Peter would glorify God. Then he said to him, "Follow me!"*

JOHN 21:19

*Also read:*

2 CORINTHIANS 4:17; HABAKKUK 3:19

# Trust Me in Difficult Circumstances

GIVE UP THE ILLUSION that you deserve a problem-free life. Part of you is still hungering for the resolution of all difficulties. This is a false hope! As I told My disciples, *in the world you will have trouble.* Link your hope not to problem solving in this life but to the promise of an eternity of problem-free life in heaven. Instead of seeking perfection in this fallen world, pour your energy into seeking Me: the Perfect One.

It is possible to enjoy Me and glorify Me in the midst of adverse circumstances. In fact, My Light shines most brightly through believers who trust Me in the dark. That kind of trust is supernatural: a production of My indwelling Spirit. When things seem all wrong, trust Me anyway. I am much less interested in right circumstances than in right responses to whatever comes your way.

> *"I have told you these things, so that in me you may*
> *have peace. In this world you will have trouble. But*
> *take heart! I have overcome the world."*
>
> JOHN 16:33
>
> *Also read:*
>
> PSALM 112:4, 7

COME TO ME FOR REST AND REFRESHMENT. The journey has been too much for you, and you are bone-weary. Do not be ashamed of your exhaustion. Instead, see it as an opportunity for Me to take charge of your life.

Remember that *I can fit everything into a pattern for good*, including the things you wish were different. Start with where you are at this point in time and space, accepting that this is where I intend you to be. You will get through today one step, one moment at a time. Your main responsibility is to remain attentive to Me, letting Me guide you through the many choices along your pathway.

This sounds like an easy assignment, but it is not. Your desire to live in My Presence goes against the grain of the world, the flesh, and the devil. Much of your weariness results from your constant battle against these opponents. However, you are on the path of My choosing, so do not give up! *Hope in Me, for you will again praise Me for the help of My Presence.*

*We are assured and know that [God being a partner in their labor] all things work together and are [fitting into a plan] for good to and for those who love God and are called according to [His] design and purpose.*

ROMANS 8:28 AMP

*Also read:*

PSALM 42.5 NASB

# You Will Have Trouble

DO NOT LONG FOR THE ABSENCE OF PROBLEMS in your life. That is an unrealistic goal since *in this world you will have trouble*. You have an eternity of problem-free living reserved for you in heaven. Rejoice in that inheritance, which no one can take away from you, but do not seek your heaven on earth.

Begin each day anticipating problems, asking Me to equip you for whatever difficulties you will encounter. The best equipping is My living Presence, *My hand that never lets go of yours*. Discuss everything with Me. Take a lighthearted view of trouble, seeing it as a challenge that you and I together can handle. Remember that I am on your side, and *I have overcome the world*.

> *"I have told you these things, so that in me you may*
> *have peace. In this world you will have trouble. But*
> *take heart! I have overcome the world."*
>
> JOHN 16:33
>
> *Also read:*
>
> ISAIAH 41:13; PHILIPPIANS 4:13

DO NOT RESIST OR RUN FROM THE DIFFICULTIES in your life. These problems are not random mistakes; they are hand-tailored blessings designed for your benefit and growth. Embrace all the circumstances that I allow in your life, trusting Me to bring good out of them. View problems as opportunities to rely more fully on Me.

When you start to feel stressed, let those feelings alert you to your need for Me. Thus, your needs become doorways to deep dependence on Me and increasing intimacy between us. Although self-sufficiency is acclaimed in the world, reliance on Me produces abundant living in My kingdom. Thank Me for the difficulties in your life since they provide protection from the idolatry of self-reliance.

> *"I am the vine; you are the branches. If a man remains in me and I in him, he will bear much fruit; apart from me you can do nothing."*
>
> JOHN 15:5

*Also read:*

2 CORINTHIANS 1:8–9; EPHESIANS 5:20

# Embracing Adversity

SEEK ME WITH YOUR WHOLE BEING. I desire to be found by you, and I orchestrate the events of your life with that purpose in mind. When things go well and you are blessed, you can feel Me smiling on you. When you encounter rough patches along your life-journey, trust that My Light is still shining upon you. My reasons for allowing these adversities may be shrouded in mystery, but My continual Presence with you is an absolute promise. Seek Me in good times; seek Me in hard times. You will find Me watching over you all the time.

> *But if from there you seek the LORD your God, you will find him if you look for him with all your heart and with all your soul.*

> DEUTERONOMY 4:29

*Also read:*

HEBREWS 10:23; PSALM 145:20; PSALM 121:7–8

GO GENTLY THROUGH THIS DAY, keeping your eyes on Me. I will open up the way before you as you take steps of trust along your path. Sometimes the way before you appears to be blocked. If you focus on the obstacle or search for a way around it, you will probably go off course. Instead, focus on Me, the Shepherd who is leading you along your life-journey. Before you know it, the "obstacle" will be behind you and you will hardly know how you passed through it.

That is the secret of success in My kingdom. Although you remain aware of the visible world around you, your primary awareness is of Me. When the road before you looks rocky, you can trust Me to get you through that rough patch. My Presence enables you to face each day with confidence.

> *"I am the good shepherd; I know my sheep and my sheep*
> *know me—just as the Father knows me and I know the*
> *Father—and I lay down my life for the sheep."*
>
> JOHN 10:14–15

*Also read:*

ISAIAH 26:7; PROVERBS 3:25–26

**LEARN TO APPRECIATE DIFFICULT DAYS.** Be stimulated by the challenges you encounter along your way. As you journey through rough terrain with Me, gain confidence from your knowledge that together we can handle anything. This knowledge is comprised of three parts: your relationship with Me, promises in the Bible, and past experiences of coping successfully during hard times.

Look back on your life, and see how I have helped you through difficult days. If you are tempted to think, "Yes, but that was then, and this is now," remember who I am! Although you and your circumstances may change dramatically, *I remain the same* throughout time and eternity. This is the basis of your confidence. In My Presence *you live and move and have your being.*

> *"So do not fear, for I am with you; do not be dismayed,*
> *for I am your God. I will strengthen you and help you;*
> *I will uphold you with my righteous right hand."*
>
> ISAIAH 41:10
>
> *Also read:*
>
> PSALM 102:27; ACTS 17:27–28

**PROBLEMS ARE PART OF LIFE.** They are inescapable, woven into the very fabric of this fallen world. You tend to go into problem-solving mode all too readily, acting as if you have the capacity to fix everything. This is a habitual response, so automatic that it bypasses your conscious thinking. Not only does this habit frustrate you, it also distances you from Me.

Do not let fixing things be your top priority. You are ever so limited in your capacity to correct all that is wrong in the world around you. Don't weigh yourself down with responsibilities that are not your own. Instead, make your relationship with Me your primary concern. Talk with Me about whatever is on your mind, seeking My perspective on the situation. Rather than trying to fix everything that comes to your attention, ask Me to show you what is truly important. Remember that you are *en route* to heaven, and let your problems fade in the Light of eternity.

> *I will instruct you and teach you in the way you should*
> *go; I will counsel you and watch over you.*
>
> PSALM 32:8

*Also read:*

LUKE 10:41–42; PHILIPPIANS 3:20–21

WHEN YOU ARE PLAGUED by a persistent problem—one that goes on and on—view it as a rich opportunity. An ongoing problem is like a tutor who is always by your side. The learning possibilities are limited only by your willingness to be teachable. In faith, thank Me for your problem. Ask Me to open your eyes and your heart to all that I am accomplishing through this difficulty. Once you have become grateful for a problem, it loses its power to drag you down. On the contrary, your thankful attitude will lift you up into heavenly places with Me. From this perspective, your difficulty can be seen as *a slight, temporary distress that is producing for you a transcendent Glory never to cease!*

> *Although the Lord gives you the bread of adversity and the water of affliction, your teachers will be hidden no more; with your own eyes you will see them. Whether you turn to the right or to the left, your ears will hear a voice behind you, saying, "This is the way; walk in it."*

ISAIAH 30:20–21

*Also read:*

EPHESIANS 5:19–20; 2 CORINTHIANS 4:17 AMP

# Anxiety

# Strength to Spare

*I AM YOUR STRENGTH AND SHIELD.* I plan out each day and have it ready for you long before you arise from bed. I also provide the strength you need each step of the way. Instead of assessing your energy level and wondering about what's on the road ahead, concentrate on staying in touch with Me. My Power flows freely into you through our open communication. Refuse to waste energy worrying, and you will have strength to spare.

Whenever you start to feel afraid, remember that I am your Shield. But unlike inanimate armor, I am always alert and active. My Presence watches over you continually, protecting you from both known and unknown dangers. Entrust yourself to My watch-care, which is the best security system available. *I am with you and will watch over you wherever you go.*

> *The LORD is my strength and my shield; my heart*
> *trusts in him, and I am helped. My heart leaps for*
> *joy and I will give thanks to him in song.*
>
> **PSALM 28:7**

*Also read:*

**MATTHEW 6:34; PSALM 56:3–4; GENESIS 28:15**

I, THE CREATOR OF THE UNIVERSE, am with you and for you. What more could you need? When you feel some lack, it is because you are not connecting with Me at a deep level. I offer abundant Life; your part is to trust Me, refusing to worry about anything.

It is not so much adverse events that make you anxious as it is your thoughts about those events. Your mind engages in efforts to take control of a situation, to bring about the result you desire. Your thoughts close in on the problem like ravenous wolves. Determined to make things go your way, you forget that I am in charge of your life. The only remedy is to switch your focus from the problem to My Presence. Stop all your striving, and watch to see what I will do. *I am the Lord!*

> *What, then, shall we say in response to this? If God is for us, who can be against us? He who did not spare his own Son, but gave him up for us all—how will he not also, along with him, graciously give us all things?*
>
> ROMANS 8:31–32

> *Also read:*
>
> MICAH 7:7; 1 CORINTHIANS 12:3

# Lighten Your Load

THE WORLD IS TOO MUCH WITH YOU, My child. Your mind leaps from problem to problem to problem, tangling your thoughts in anxious knots. When you think like that, you leave Me out of your worldview and your mind becomes darkened. Though I yearn to help, I will not violate your freedom. I stand silently in the background of your mind, waiting for you to remember that I am with you.

When you turn from your problems to My Presence, your load is immediately lighter. Circumstances may not have changed, but we carry your burdens together. Your compulsion to "fix" everything gives way to deep, satisfying connection with Me. Together we can handle whatever this day brings.

> *"So do not fear, for I am with you; do not be dismayed,*
> *for I am your God. I will strengthen you and help you;*
> *I will uphold you with my righteous right hand."*

ISAIAH 41:10

*Also read:*

ZEPHANIAH 3:17; PSALM 34:19

I AM ALL AROUND YOU, like a cocoon of Light. My Presence with you is a promise, independent of your awareness of Me. Many things can block this awareness, but the major culprit is worry. My children tend to accept worry as an inescapable fact of life. However, worry is a form of unbelief; it is anathema to Me.

Who is in charge of your life? If it is you, then you have good reason to worry. But since I am in charge, worry is both unnecessary and counterproductive. When you start to feel anxious about something, relinquish the situation to Me. Back off a bit, redirecting your focus to Me. I will either take care of the problem Myself or show you how to handle it. In this world you will have problems, but you need not lose sight of Me.

> *"I have told you these things, so that in me you may*
> *have peace. In this world you will have trouble. But*
> *take heart! I have overcome the world."*
>
> JOHN 16:33

> *Also read:*
>
> LUKE 12:22–31

# Choose to Trust

*DO NOT WORRY ABOUT TOMORROW!* This is not a suggestion but a command. I divided time into days and nights so that you would have manageable portions of life to handle. *My grace is sufficient for you*, but its sufficiency is for only one day at a time. When you worry about the future, you heap day upon day of troubles onto your flimsy frame. You stagger under this heavy load, which I never intended you to carry.

Throw off this oppressive burden with one quick thrust of trust. Anxious thoughts meander about and crisscross in your brain, but trusting Me brings you directly into My Presence. As you thus affirm your faith, shackles of worry fall off instantly. Enjoy My Presence continually by trusting Me at all times.

> *"Therefore do not worry about tomorrow, for tomorrow will worry about itself. Each day has enough trouble of its own."*
>
> MATTHEW 6:34

*Also read:*

2 CORINTHIANS 12:9; PSALM 62:8 NKJV

# Attitude

# Today Is a Gift

**TRY TO VIEW EACH DAY** as an adventure, carefully planned out by your Guide. Instead of staring into the day that is ahead of you, attempting to program it according to your will, be attentive to Me and to all I have prepared for you. Thank Me for this day of life, recognizing that it is a precious, unrepeatable gift. Trust that I am with you each moment, whether you sense My Presence or not. A thankful, trusting attitude helps you to see events in your life from My perspective.

A life lived close to Me will never be dull or predictable. Expect each day to contain surprises! Resist your tendency to search for the easiest route through the day. Be willing to follow wherever I lead. No matter how steep or treacherous the path before you, the safest place to be is by My side.

*This is the day the LORD has made;*
*We will rejoice and be glad in it.*

PSALM 118:24 NKJV

*Also read:*

ISAIAH 41:10; 1 PETER 2:21

*THIS IS THE DAY THAT I HAVE MADE. Rejoice and be glad in it.* Begin the day with open hands of faith, ready to receive all that I am pouring into this brief portion of your life. Be careful not to complain about anything, even the weather, since I am the Author of your circumstances. The best way to handle unwanted situations is to thank Me for them. This act of faith frees you from resentment and frees Me to work My ways into the situation so that good emerges from it.

To find Joy in this day, you must live within its boundaries. I knew what I was doing when I divided time into twenty-four-hour segments. I understand human frailty, and I know that you can bear the weight of only one day at a time. Do not worry about tomorrow or get stuck in the past. There is abundant Life in My Presence today.

*This is the day the LORD has made; let us rejoice and be glad in it.*

PSALM 118:24

*Also read:*

PHILIPPIANS 3:13–14; HEBREWS 3:13

# Live a Life of Thankfulness

I AM CALLING YOU to a life of thankfulness. I want all your moments to be punctuated with thanksgiving. The basis for your gratitude is My sovereignty. I am the Creator and Controller of the universe. Heaven and earth are filled with My glorious Presence.

When you criticize or complain, you are acting as if you think you could run the world better than I do. From your limited human perspective, it may look as if I'm mismanaging things. But you don't know what I know or see what I see. If I pulled back the curtain to allow you to view heavenly realms, you would understand much more. However, I have designed you to *live by faith*, not by sight. I lovingly shield you from knowing the future or seeing into the spirit world. Acknowledge My sovereignty by *giving thanks in all circumstances*.

> *And they were calling to one another: "Holy, holy, holy is the LORD Almighty; the whole earth is full of his glory."*
>
> ISAIAH 6:3

*Also read:*

2 CORINTHIANS 5:7; 1 THESSALONIANS 5:18

# When Things Don't Go as Planned

WHEN THINGS DON'T GO AS YOU WOULD LIKE, accept the situation immediately. If you indulge in feelings of regret, they can easily spill over the line into resentment. Remember that I am sovereign over your circumstances, and *humble yourself under My mighty hand*. Rejoice in what I am doing in your life, even though it is beyond your understanding.

*I am the Way, the Truth, and the Life.* In Me you have everything you need, both for this life and for the life yet to come. Don't let the impact of the world shatter your thinking or draw you away from focusing on Me. The ultimate challenge is to keep fixing your eyes on Me, no matter what is going on around you. When I am central in your thinking, you are able to view circumstances from My perspective.

> *Young men, in the same way be submissive to those who are older. All of you, clothe yourselves with humility toward one another, because, "God opposes the proud but gives grace to the humble." Humble yourselves, therefore, under God's mighty hand, that he may lift you up in due time.*

1 PETER 5:5–6

*Also read:*

JOHN 14:6

# There Is a Better Way

LET ME HELP YOU GET THROUGH THIS DAY. There are many possible paths to travel between your getting up in the morning and your lying down at night. Stay alert to the many choice-points along the way, being continually aware of My Presence. You will get through this day one way or the other. One way is to moan and groan, stumbling along with shuffling feet. This will get you to the end of the day eventually, but there is a better way. You can choose to walk with Me along the path of Peace, leaning on Me as much as you need. There will still be difficulties along the way, but you can face them confidently in My strength. Thank Me for each problem you encounter, and watch to see how I transform trials into blessings.

*And do not grumble, as some of them did—
and were killed by the destroying angel.*

1 CORINTHIANS 10:10

*Also read:*

LUKE 1:79; 2 SAMUEL 22:29–30

THANK ME FOR THE VERY THINGS that are troubling you. You are on the brink of rebellion, precariously close to shaking your fist in My Face. You are tempted to indulge in just a little complaining about My treatment of you. But once you step over that line, torrents of rage and self-pity can sweep you away. The best protection against this indulgence is thanksgiving. It is impossible to thank Me and curse Me at the same time.

Thanking Me for trials will feel awkward and contrived at first. But if you persist, your thankful words, prayed in faith, will eventually make a difference in your heart. Thankfulness awakens you to My Presence, which overshadows all your problems.

*I will offer to You the sacrifice of thanksgiving,*
*And will call upon the name of the LORD.*

PSALM 116:17 NKJV

*Also read:*

PHILIPPIANS 4:4–6; PSALM 100:2 NKJV

# Savor Every Blessing

**LEARN TO ENJOY LIFE MORE.** Relax, remembering that I am *God with you*. I crafted you with enormous capacity to know Me and enjoy My Presence. When My people wear sour faces and walk through their lives with resigned rigidity, I am displeased. When you walk through a day with childlike delight, savoring every blessing, you proclaim your trust in Me, your ever-present Shepherd. The more you focus on My Presence with you, the more fully you can enjoy life. Glorify Me through your pleasure in Me. Thus you proclaim My Presence to the watching world.

> *"The virgin will be with child and will give birth to a son, and they will call him Immanuel"—which means, "God with us."*
>
> **MATTHEW 1:23**

*Also read:*

**JOHN 10:10–11; JUDE vv. 24–25**

WHEN MANY THINGS SEEM TO BE GOING WRONG, trust Me. When your life feels increasingly out of control, thank Me. These are supernatural responses, and they can lift you above your circumstances. If you do what comes naturally in the face of difficulties, you may fall prey to negativism. Even a few complaints can set you on a path that is a downward spiral, by darkening your perspective and mind-set. With this attitude controlling you, complaints flow more and more readily from your mouth. Each one moves you steadily down the slippery spiral. The lower you go, the faster you slide; but it is still possible to apply brakes. Cry out to Me in My Name! Affirm your trust in Me, regardless of how you feel. Thank Me for everything, though this seems unnatural—even irrational. Gradually you will begin to ascend, recovering your lost ground.

When you are back on ground level, you can face your circumstances from a humble perspective. If you choose supernatural responses this time—trusting and thanking Me—you will experience My unfathomable Peace.

*But I trust in your unfailing love; my heart rejoices in your salvation.*

PSALM 13:5

*Also read:*

EPHESIANS 5:20; PSALM 34:10

# A Safe Place

YOU HAVE BEEN ON A LONG, UPHILL JOURNEY, and your energy is almost spent. Though you have faltered at times, you have not let go of My hand. I am pleased with your desire to stay close to Me. There is one thing, however, that displeases Me: your tendency to complain. You may talk to Me as much as you like about the difficulty of the path we are following. I understand better than anyone else the stresses and strains that have afflicted you. You can ventilate safely to Me because talking with Me tempers your thoughts and helps you see things from My perspective.

Complaining to others is another matter altogether. It opens the door to deadly sins such as self-pity and rage. Whenever you are tempted to grumble, come to Me and talk it out. As you open up to Me, I will put My thoughts in your mind and My song in your heart.

*"I will refresh the weary and satisfy the faint."*

JEREMIAH 31:25

*Also read:*

PHILIPPIANS 2:14–15; PSALM 40:3

# Freedom from Resentment

**TO LIVE IN MY PRESENCE CONSISTENTLY**, you must expose and expel your rebellious tendencies. When something interferes with your plans or desires, you tend to resent the interference. Try to become aware of each resentment, however petty it may seem. Don't push those unpleasant feelings down; instead, let them come to the surface where you can deal with them. Ask My Spirit to increase your awareness of resentful feelings. Bring them boldly into the Light of My Presence so that I can free you from them.

The ultimate solution to rebellious tendencies is submission to My authority over you. Intellectually, you rejoice in My sovereignty, without which the world would be a terrifying place. But when My sovereign will encroaches on your little domain of control, you often react with telltale resentment.

The best response to losses or thwarted hopes is praise: *The Lord gives and the Lord takes away. Blessed be the name of the Lord.* Remember that all good things—your possessions, your family and friends, your health and abilities, your time—are gifts from Me. Instead of feeling entitled to all these blessings, respond to them with gratitude. Be prepared to let go of anything I take from you, but never let go of My hand!

> *Humble yourselves, therefore, under God's mighty*
> *hand, that he may lift you up in due time.*
>
> 1 PETER 5:6

*Also read:*

PSALM 139:23–24; JOB 1:21 NKJV

# Change

I AM THE RISEN ONE who shines upon you always. You worship a living Deity, not some idolatrous, man-made image. Your relationship with Me is meant to be vibrant and challenging, as I invade more and more areas of your life. Do not fear change, for I am making you a *new creation, with old things passing away and new things continually on the horizon.* When you cling to old ways and sameness, you resist My work within you. I want you to embrace all that I am doing in your life, finding your security in Me alone.

It is easy to make an idol of routine, finding security within the boundaries you build around your life. Although each day contains twenty-four hours, every single one presents a unique set of circumstances. Don't try to force-fit today into yesterday's mold. Instead, ask Me to open your eyes so you can find all I have prepared for you in this precious day of Life.

> *The angel said to the women, "Do not be afraid, for I know that you are looking for Jesus, who was crucified."*
>
> MATTHEW 28:5

> *Also read:*
>
> 2 CORINTHIANS 5:17

# Letting Go

THIS IS A TIME IN YOUR LIFE when you must learn to let go: of loved ones, of possessions, of control. In order to let go of something that is precious to you, you need to rest in My Presence, where you are complete. Take time to bask in the Light of My Love. As you relax more and more, your grasping hand gradually opens up, releasing your prized possession into My care.

You can feel secure, even in the midst of cataclysmic changes, through awareness of My continual Presence. The One who never leaves you is the same One who never changes: *I am the same yesterday, today, and forever.* As you release more and more things into My care, remember that I never let go of your hand. Herein lies your security, which no one and no circumstance can take from you.

*Blessed are those who have learned to acclaim you,*
*who walk in the light of your presence, O LORD.*

PSALM 89:15

*Also read:*

HEBREWS 13:8; ISAIAH 41:13

*TRUST ME, AND DON'T BE AFRAID.* Many things feel out of control. Your routines are not running smoothly. You tend to feel more secure when your life is predictable. Let Me lead you to *the rock that is higher than you* and your circumstances. *Take refuge in the shelter of My wings*, where you are absolutely secure.

When you are shaken out of your comfortable routines, grip My hand tightly and look for growth opportunities. Instead of bemoaning the loss of your comfort, accept the challenge of something new. *I lead you on from glory to glory*, making you fit for My kingdom. Say *yes* to the ways I work in your life. Trust Me, and don't be afraid.

> *Surely God is my salvation; I will trust and not*
> *be afraid. The Lord, the Lord, is my strength*
> *and my song; he has become my salvation.*
>
> ISAIAH 12:2
>
> *Also read:*
>
> PSALM 61:2–4; 2 CORINTHIANS 3:18 NKJV

# Make Me Your Focal Point

MAKE ME YOUR FOCAL POINT as you move through this day. Just as a spinning ballerina must keep returning her eyes to a given point to maintain her balance, so you must keep returning your focus to Me. Circumstances are in flux, and the world seems to be whirling around you. The only way to keep your balance is to *fix your eyes on Me*, the One who never changes. If you gaze too long at your circumstances, you will become dizzy and confused. Look to Me, refreshing yourself in My Presence, and your steps will be steady and sure.

*Let us fix our eyes on Jesus, the author and perfecter of our faith,*
*who for the joy set before him endured the cross, scorning its*
*shame, and sat down at the right hand of the throne of God.*

HEBREWS 12:2

*Also read:*

PSALM 102:27; 1 JOHN 3:19–20

# The One Who Never Changes

IN A WORLD OF UNRELENTING CHANGES, I am the One who never changes. *I am the Alpha and the Omega, the First and the Last, the Beginning and the End.* Find in Me the stability for which you have yearned.

I created a beautifully ordered world: one that reflects My perfection. Now, however, the world is under the bondage of sin and evil. Every person on the planet faces gaping jaws of uncertainty. The only antidote to this poisonous threat is drawing closer to Me. In My Presence you can face uncertainty with perfect Peace.

> *"I am the Alpha and the Omega, the First and the Last, the Beginning and the End."*
>
> REVELATION 22:13

*Also read:*

ROMANS 5:12; JOHN 16:33 AMP

# Dependence

I WANT YOU TO BE ALL MINE. I am weaning you from other dependencies. Your security rests in Me alone—not in other people, not in circumstances. Depending only on Me may feel like walking on a tightrope, but there is a safety net underneath: *the everlasting arms.* So don't be afraid of falling. Instead, look ahead to Me. I am always before you, beckoning you on— one step at a time. *Neither height nor depth, nor anything else in all creation, can separate you from My loving Presence.*

*The eternal God is your refuge, and underneath are the everlasting arms. He will drive out your enemy before you, saying, "Destroy him!"*

DEUTERONOMY 33:27

*Also read:*

PROVERBS 16:9; ROMANS 8:38–39

# Declaration of Dependence

HOLD MY HAND—AND TRUST. So long as you are conscious of My Presence with you, all is well. It is virtually impossible to stumble while walking in the Light with Me. I designed you to enjoy Me above all else. You find the deepest fulfillment of your heart in Me alone.

Fearful, anxious thoughts melt away in the Light of My Presence. When you turn away from Me, you are vulnerable to the darkness that is always at work in the world. Don't be surprised by how easily you sin when you forget to cling to My hand. In the world, dependency is seen as immaturity. But in My kingdom, dependence on Me is a prime measure of maturity.

*"So do not fear, for I am with you; do not be dismayed,
for I am your God. I will strengthen you and help you;
I will uphold you with my righteous right hand."*

ISAIAH 41:10

*Also read:*

EPHESIANS 5:8 NKJV; PSALM 62:5–6

# Use Your Freedom Wisely

DO EVERYTHING IN DEPENDENCE ON ME. The desire to act independently—apart from Me—springs from the root of pride. Self-sufficiency is subtle, insinuating its way into your thoughts and actions without your realizing it. But *apart from Me, you can do nothing*: that is, nothing of eternal value. My deepest desire for you is that you learn to depend on Me in every situation. I move heaven and earth to accomplish this purpose, but you must collaborate with Me in this training. Teaching you would be simple if I negated your free will or overwhelmed you with My Power. However, I love you too much to withdraw the godlike privilege I bestowed on you as My image-bearer. Use your freedom wisely by relying on Me constantly. Thus you enjoy My Presence and My Peace.

> *"I am the vine; you are the branches. If a man remains in me and I in him, he will bear much fruit; apart from me you can do nothing."*
>
> JOHN 15:5

*Also read:*

EPHESIANS 6:10; GENESIS 1:26–27

# True Confidence

COME TO ME WHEN YOU ARE HURTING, and I will soothe your pain. Come to Me when you are joyful, and I will share your Joy, multiplying it many times over. I am All you need, just when you need it. Your deepest desires find fulfillment in Me alone.

This is the age of self-help. Bookstores abound with books about "taking care of number one," making oneself the center of all things. The main goal of these methodologies is to become self-sufficient and confident. You, however, have been called to take a "road less traveled": continual dependence on Me. True confidence comes from knowing you are complete in My Presence. Everything you need has its counterpart in Me.

*Shout for joy, O heavens; rejoice, O earth; burst into song, O mountains! For the LORD comforts his people and will have compassion on his afflicted ones.*

ISAIAH 49:13

*Also read:*

JOHN 15:5; JAMES 1:4

# Direction

# One Step at a Time

**YOU CAN ACHIEVE THE VICTORIOUS LIFE** through living in deep dependence on Me. People usually associate victory with success: not falling or stumbling, not making mistakes. But those who are successful in their own strength tend to go their own way, forgetting about Me. It is through problems and failure, weakness and neediness, that you learn to rely on Me.

True dependence is not simply asking Me to bless what you have decided to do. It is coming to Me with an open mind and heart, inviting Me to plant My desires within you. I may infuse within you a dream that seems far beyond your reach. You know that in yourself you cannot achieve such a goal. Thus begins your journey of profound reliance on Me. It is a faith-walk, taken one step at a time, leaning on Me as much as you need. This is not a path of continual success but of multiple failures. However, each failure is followed by a growth spurt, nourished by increased reliance on Me. Enjoy the blessedness of a victorious life through deepening your dependence on Me.

*The righteous cry out, and the LORD hears them; he delivers*
*them from all their troubles. The LORD is close to the*
*brokenhearted and saves those who are crushed in spirit.*

PSALM 34:17–18

*Also read:*

2 CORINTHIANS 5:7 NKJV

APPROACH THIS DAY WITH AWARENESS of who is Boss. As you make plans for the day, remember that it is I who orchestrates the events of your life. On days when things go smoothly, according to your plans, you may be unaware of My sovereign Presence. On days when your plans are thwarted, be on the lookout for Me! I may be doing something important in your life, something quite different from what you expected. It is essential at such times to stay in communication with Me, accepting My way as better than yours. Don't try to figure out what is happening. Simply trust Me and thank Me in advance for the good that will come out of it all. *I know the plans I have for you, and they are good.*

> *"As the heavens are higher than the earth, so are my ways higher than your ways and my thoughts than your thoughts. As the rain and the snow come down from heaven, and do not return to it without watering the earth and making it bud and flourish, so that it yields seed for the sower and bread for the eater, so is my word that goes out from my mouth: It will not return to me empty, but will accomplish what I desire and achieve the purpose for which I sent it."*

ISAIAH 55:9–11

*Also read:*

JEREMIAH 29:11

# Falling into Place

**SAVE YOUR BEST STRIVING FOR SEEKING MY FACE.** I am constantly communicating with you. To find Me and hear My voice, you must seek Me above all else. Anything that you desire more than Me becomes an idol. When you are determined to get your own way, you blot Me out of your consciousness. Instead of single-mindedly pursuing some goal, talk with Me about it. Let the Light of My Presence shine on this pursuit so that you can see it from My perspective. If the goal fits into My plans for you, I will help you reach it. If it is contrary to My will for you, I will gradually change the desire of your heart. *Seek Me first* and foremost; then the rest of your life will fall into place, piece by piece.

*Look to the LORD and his strength; seek his face always.*

**1 CHRONICLES 16:11**

*Also read:*

**PROVERBS 19:21 NKJV; MATTHEW 6:33**

WAITING ON ME MEANS DIRECTING your attention to Me in hopeful anticipation of what I will do. It entails trusting Me with every fiber of your being instead of trying to figure things out yourself. Waiting on Me is the way I designed you to live: all day, every day. I created you to stay conscious of Me as you go about your daily duties.

I have promised many blessings to those who wait on Me: *renewed strength*, living above one's circumstances, resurgence of hope, awareness of My continual Presence. Waiting on Me enables you to glorify Me by living in deep dependence on Me, ready to do My will. It also helps you to enjoy Me; *in My Presence is fullness of Joy.*

> *I say to myself, "The LORD is my portion; therefore I will wait for him." The LORD is good to those whose hope is in him, to the one who seeks him; it is good to wait quietly for the salvation of the LORD.*

LAMENTATIONS 3:24–26

*Also read:*

ISAIAH 40:31; PSALM 16:11 NKJV

# Delighting in the Everyday

WHEN I GIVE YOU NO SPECIAL GUIDANCE, stay where you are. Concentrate on doing your everyday tasks in awareness of My Presence with you. The Joy of My Presence will shine on you, as you do everything for Me. Thus you invite Me into every aspect of your life. Through collaborating with Me in all things, you allow My Life to merge with yours. This is the secret of not only joyful living but of victorious living. I designed you to depend on Me moment by moment, recognizing that *apart from Me you can do nothing.*

Be thankful for quiet days, when nothing special seems to be happening. Instead of being bored by the lack of action, use times of routine to seek My Face. Although this is an invisible transaction, it speaks volumes in spiritual realms. Moreover, you are richly blessed when you walk trustingly with Me through the routines of your day.

> *Whatever you do, work at it with all your heart,*
> *as working for the Lord, not for men.*
>
> COLOSSIANS 3:23

*Also read:*

JOHN 15:5; PSALM 105:4

**DO NOT SEARCH FOR SECURITY IN THE WORLD** you inhabit. You tend to make mental checklists of things you need to do in order to gain control of your life. If only you could check everything off your list, you could relax and be at peace. But the more you work to accomplish that goal, the more things crop up on your list. The harder you try, the more frustrated you become.

There is a better way to find security in this life. Instead of scrutinizing your checklist, focus your attention on My Presence with you. This continual contact with Me will keep you in My Peace. Moreover, I will help you sort out what is important and what is not, what needs to be done now and what does not. *Fix your eyes not on what is seen* (your circumstances), *but on what is unseen* (My Presence).

*Therefore, holy brothers, who share in the heavenly calling, fix your thoughts on Jesus, the apostle and high priest whom we confess.*

HEBREWS 3:1

*Also read:*

ISAIAH 26:3 NKJV; 2 CORINTHIANS 4:18

# God's Way Is Perfect

**I AM INVOLVED IN EACH MOMENT OF YOUR LIFE.** I have carefully mapped out every inch of your journey through this day, even though much of it may feel haphazard. Because the world is in a fallen condition, things always seem to be unraveling around the edges. Expect to find trouble in this day. At the same time, trust that *My way is perfect*, even in the midst of such messy imperfection.

Stay conscious of Me as you go through this day, remembering that I never leave your side. Let the Holy Spirit guide you step by step, protecting you from unnecessary trials and equipping you to get through whatever must be endured. As you trudge through the sludge of this fallen world, keep your mind in heavenly places with Me. Thus the Light of My Presence shines on you, giving you Peace and Joy that circumstances cannot touch.

> *As for God, his way is perfect; the word of the LORD is flawless. He is a shield for all who take refuge in him.*
>
> **PSALM 18:30**

> *Also read:*
>
> **ISAIAH 41:13; PSALM 36:9**

**KEEP WALKING WITH ME ALONG THE PATH** I have chosen for you. Your desire to live close to Me is a delight to My heart. I could instantly grant you the spiritual riches you desire, but that is not My way for you. Together we will forge a pathway up the high mountain. The journey is arduous at times, and you are weak. Someday you will dance light-footed on the high peaks; but for now your walk is often plodding and heavy. All I require of you is to take the next step, clinging to My hand for strength and direction. Though the path is difficult and the scenery dull at the moment, there are sparkling surprises just around the bend. Stay on the path I have selected for you. It is truly the *path of Life*.

*But those who wait on the LORD shall renew their strength;*
*they shall mount up with wings like eagles, they shall run*
*and not be weary, they shall walk and not faint.*

ISAIAH 40:31 NKJV

*Also read:*

PSALM 37:23–24; PSALM 16:11 NKJV

# Baby Steps of Trust

POUR ALL OF YOUR ENERGY into trusting Me. It is through trust that you stay connected to Me, aware of My Presence. Every step on your life-journey can be a step of faith. Baby steps of trust are simple for you; you can take them with almost unconscious ease. Giant steps are another matter altogether: leaping across chasms in semidarkness, scaling cliffs of uncertainty, *trudging through the valley of the shadow of death*. These feats require sheer concentration, as well as utter commitment to Me.

Each of My children is a unique blend of temperament, giftedness, and life experiences. Something that is a baby step for you may be a giant step for another person, and vice versa. Only I know the difficulty or ease of each segment of your journey. Beware of trying to impress others by acting as if your giant steps are only baby ones. Do not judge others who hesitate in trembling fear before an act that would be easy for you. If each of My children would seek to please Me above all else, fear of others' judgments would vanish, as would attempts to impress others. Focus your attention on the path just ahead of you and on the One who never leaves your side.

*Even though I walk through the valley of the shadow*
*of death, I will fear no evil, for you are with me;*
*your rod and your staff, they comfort me.*

PSALM 23:4

*Also read:*

MATTHEW 7:1–2; PROVERBS 29:25

# Waiting for Direction

WALK PEACEFULLY WITH ME THROUGH THIS DAY. You are wondering how you will cope with all that is expected of you. You must traverse this day like any other: one step at a time. Instead of mentally rehearsing how you will do this or that, keep your mind on My Presence and on taking the next step. The more demanding your day, the more help you can expect from Me. This is a training opportunity, since I designed you for deep dependence on your Shepherd-King. Challenging times wake you up and amplify your awareness of needing My help.

When you don't know what to do, wait while I open the way before you. Trust that I know what I'm doing, and be ready to follow My lead. *I will give strength to you, and I will bless you with Peace.*

*The LORD replied, "My Presence will go with you, and I will give you rest."*

EXODUS 33:14

*Also read:*

DEUTERONOMY 33:25; HEBREWS 13:20–21; PSALM 29:11

# Expect to See Miracles

MY PLAN FOR YOUR LIFE IS UNFOLDING before you. Sometimes the road you are traveling seems blocked, or it opens up so painfully slowly that you must hold yourself back. Then, when the time is right, the way before you suddenly clears—through no effort of your own. What you have longed for and worked for I present to you freely, as pure gift. You feel awed by the ease with which I operate in the world, and you glimpse *My Power and My Glory.*

Do not fear your weakness, for it is the stage on which My Power and Glory perform most brilliantly. As you persevere along the path I have prepared for you, depending on My strength to sustain you, expect to see miracles—and you will. Miracles are not always visible to the naked eye, but those who *live by faith* can see them clearly. *Living by faith, rather than sight*, enables you to see My Glory.

> *I have seen you in the sanctuary and beheld your power and your glory. Because your love is better than life, my lips will glorify you. I will praise you as long as I live, and in your name I will lift up my hands. My soul will be satisfied as with the richest of foods; with singing lips my mouth will praise you.*
>
> PSALM 63:2–5
>
> *Also read:*
>
> 2 CORINTHIANS 5:7; JOHN 11:40

# Discerning God's Will

# Listen Closely

I LOVE YOU FOR WHO YOU ARE, not for what you do. Many voices vie for control of your mind, especially when you sit in silence. You must learn to discern what is My voice and what is not. Ask My Spirit to give you this discernment. Many of My children run around in circles, trying to obey the various voices directing their lives. This results in fragmented, frustrating patterns of living. Do not fall into this trap. Walk closely with Me each moment, listening for My directives and enjoying My Companionship. Refuse to let other voices tie you up in knots. *My sheep know My voice and follow Me wherever I lead.*

> *As a prisoner for the Lord, then, I urge you to live a life worthy of the calling you have received. Be completely humble and gentle; be patient, bearing with one another in love. Make every effort to keep the unity of the Spirit through the bond of peace. There is one body and one Spirit—just as you were called to one hope when you were called—one Lord, one faith, one baptism; one God and Father of all, who is over all and through all and in all.*
>
> EPHESIANS 4:1–6
>
> *Also read:*
>
> JOHN 10:4

STOP TRYING TO WORK THINGS OUT before their times have come. Accept the limitations of living one day at a time. When something comes to your attention, ask Me whether or not it is part of today's agenda. If it isn't, release it into My care and go on about today's duties. When you follow this practice, there will be a beautiful simplicity about your life: *a time for everything, and everything in its time.*

A life lived close to Me is not complicated or cluttered. When your focus is on My Presence, many things that once troubled you lose their power over you. Though the world around you is messy and confusing, remember that *I have overcome the world. I have told you these things, so that in Me you may have Peace.*

*There is a time for everything, and a season*
*for every activity under heaven.*

ECCLESIASTES 3:1

*Also read:*

ECCLESIASTES 8:6–7; JOHN 16:33

# One Choice at a Time

AS YOU LOOK INTO THE DAY that stretches out before you, you see many choice-points along the way. The myriad possibilities these choices present can confuse you. Draw your mind back to the threshold of this day, where I stand beside you, lovingly preparing you for what is ahead.

You must make your choices one at a time since each is contingent upon the decision that precedes it. Instead of trying to create a mental map of your path through this day, focus on My loving Presence with you. I will equip you as you go so that you can handle whatever comes your way. Trust Me to supply what you need when you need it.

> *Because of the LORD's great love we are not consumed, for*
> *his compassions never fail. They are new every morning;*
> *great is your faithfulness. I say to myself, "The LORD is my*
> *portion; therefore I will wait for him." The LORD is good*
> *to those whose hope is in him, to the one who seeks him; it*
> *is good to wait quietly for the salvation of the LORD.*
>
> ### LAMENTATIONS 3:22–26
>
> *Also read:*
>
> ### PROVERBS 16:9; PSALM 34:8 NKJV

I AM YOUR LORD! Seek Me as Friend and Lover of your soul, but remember that I am also King of kings—sovereign over all. You can make some plans as you gaze into the day that stretches out before you. But you need to hold those plans tentatively, anticipating that I may have other ideas. The most important thing to determine is what to do right now. Instead of scanning the horizon of your life, looking for things that need to be done, concentrate on the task before you and the One who never leaves your side. Let everything else fade into the background. This will unclutter your mind, allowing Me to occupy more and more of your consciousness.

Trust Me to show you what to do when you have finished what you are doing now. I will guide you step by step as you bend your will to Mine. Thus you stay close to Me on the *path of Peace*.

*"They will make war against the Lamb, but the Lamb will overcome them because he is Lord of lords and King of kings— and with him will be his called, chosen and faithful followers."*

REVELATION 17:14

*Also read:*

PROVERBS 19:21; LUKE 1:79

# Your Unique Path

STAY ON THE HIGH ROAD WITH ME. Many voices clamor for your attention, trying to divert you to another path. But I have called you to walk ever so closely with Me, soaking in My Presence, living in My Peace. This is My unique design for you, planned before the world began.

I have called each of My children to a different path, distinctly designed for that one. Do not let anyone convince you that his path is the only right way. And be careful not to extol your path as superior to another's way. What I require of you is *to act justly, to love mercy, and to walk humbly with Me*—wherever I lead.

> *"Peace I leave with you, My peace I give to you;*
> *not as the world gives do I give to you. Let not your*
> *heart be troubled, neither let it be afraid."*
>
> JOHN 14:27 NKJV

*Also read:*

EPHESIANS 2:10; MICAH 6:8

# The Responsibility of Free Will

SEEK TO PLEASE ME ABOVE ALL ELSE. Let that goal be your focal point as you go through this day. Such a mind-set will protect you from scattering your energy to the winds. The free will I bestowed on you comes with awesome responsibility. Each day presents you with choice after choice. Many of these decisions you ignore and thus make by default. Without a focal point to guide you, you can easily lose your way. That's why it is so important to stay in communication with Me, living in thankful awareness of My Presence.

You inhabit a fallen, disjointed world, where things are constantly unraveling around the edges. Only a vibrant relationship with Me can keep you from coming unraveled too.

*"But seek first his kingdom and his righteousness, and all these things will be given to you as well."*

MATTHEW 6:33

*Also read:*

JOHN 8:29; COLOSSIANS 3:23–24

# Get Out of That Rut

AS YOU BECOME INCREASINGLY AWARE of My Presence, you find it easier to discern the way you should go. This is one of the practical benefits of living close to Me. Instead of wondering about what is on the road ahead or worrying about what you should do if . . . or when . . . , you can concentrate on staying in communication with Me. When you actually arrive at a choice-point, I will show you which direction to go.

Many people are so preoccupied with future plans and decisions that they fail to see choices they need to make today. Without any conscious awareness, they make their habitual responses. People who live this way find a dullness creeping into their lives. They sleepwalk through their days, following well-worn paths of routine.

I, the Creator of the universe, am the most creative Being imaginable. I will not leave you circling in deeply rutted paths. Instead, I will lead you along fresh trails of adventure, revealing to you things you did not know. Stay in communication with Me. Follow My guiding Presence.

*I will instruct you and teach you in the way you should go; I will counsel you and watch over you.*

PSALM 32:8

*Also read:*

GENESIS 1:1; ISAIAH 58:11 NKJV

SEEK TO PLEASE ME ABOVE ALL ELSE. As you journey through today, there will be many choice-points along your way. Most of the day's decisions will be small ones you have to make quickly. You need some rule of thumb to help you make good choices. Many people's decisions are a combination of their habitual responses and their desire to please themselves or others. This is not My way for you. Strive to please Me in everything, not just in major decisions. This is possible only to the extent that you are living in close communion with Me. When My Presence is your deepest delight, you know almost instinctively what will please Me. A quick *glance* at Me is all you need to make the right choice. *Delight yourself in Me* more and more; seek My pleasure in all you do.

> *"The one who sent me is with me; he has not left me*
> *alone, for I always do what pleases him."*
>
> JOHN 8:29

*Also read:*

HEBREWS 11:5–6; PSALM 37:4

# The Path of Freedom

**THERE IS NO CONDEMNATION** for those who are in Me. *The law of the Spirit of Life has set you free from the law of sin and death.* Not many Christians know how to live in this radical freedom, which is their birthright. I died to set you free; live freely in Me!

To walk along the path of freedom, you must keep your mind firmly fixed on Me. Many voices proclaim, "This is the way for you to go," but only My voice tells you the true way. If you follow the way of the world with all its glitter and glamour, you will descend deeper and deeper into an abyss. Christian voices also can lead you astray: "Do this!" "Don't do that!" "Pray this way!" "Don't pray that way!" If you listen to all those voices, you will become increasingly confused.

Be content to be a simple sheep, listening for My voice and following Me. *I will lead you into restful green pastures and guide you along paths of righteousness.*

> *Therefore, there is now no condemnation for those who are in Christ Jesus, because through Christ Jesus the law of the Spirit of life set me free from the law of sin and death.*
>
> ROMANS 8:1–2

*Also read:*

ISAIAH 30:21; JOHN 10:27; PSALM 23:1–3

# Distractions

# Greater Than Any Gift

BE STILL IN MY PRESENCE even though countless tasks clamor for your attention. Nothing is as important as spending time with Me. While you wait in My Presence, I do My best work within you, *transforming you by the renewing of your mind*. If you skimp on this time with Me, you may plunge headlong into the wrong activities, missing the richness of what I have planned for you.

Do not seek Me primarily for what I can give you. Remember that I, the Giver, am infinitely greater than any gift I might impart to you. Though I delight in blessing My children, I am deeply grieved when My blessings become idols in their hearts. Anything can be an idol if it distracts you from Me as your *First Love*. When I am the ultimate Desire of your heart, you are safe from the danger of idolatry. As you wait in My Presence, enjoy the greatest gift of all: *Christ in you, the hope of Glory*!

*Do not conform any longer to the pattern of this world,*
*but be transformed by the renewing of your mind.*
*Then you will be able to test and approve what God's*
*will is—his good, pleasing and perfect will.*

ROMANS 12:2

*Also read:*

REVELATION 2:4; COLOSSIANS 1:27

**LISTEN TO ME CONTINUALLY.** I have much to communicate to you, so many people and situations in need of prayer. I am training you to set your mind on Me more and more, tuning out distractions through the help of My Spirit.

Walk with Me in holy trust, responding to My initiatives rather than trying to make things fit your plans. I died to set you free, and that includes freedom from compulsive planning. When your mind spins with a multitude of thoughts, you cannot hear My voice. A mind preoccupied with planning pays homage to the idol of control. Turn from this idolatry back to Me. Listen to Me and live abundantly!

> *Trust in Him at all times, you people; pour out your heart before Him; God is a refuge for us.*
>
> **PSALM 62:8 NKJV**

*Also read:*

**JOHN 8:36; PROVERBS 19:21; JOHN 10:27**

# The Loftiest Goal

DO NOT BE DISCOURAGED by the difficulty of keeping your focus on Me. I know that your heart's desire is to be aware of My Presence continually. This is a lofty goal; you aim toward it but never fully achieve it in this life. Don't let feelings of failure weigh you down. Instead, try to see yourself as I see you. First of all, I am delighted by your deep desire to walk closely with Me through your life. I am pleased each time you initiate communication with Me. In addition, I notice the progress you have made since you first resolved to live in My Presence.

When you realize that your mind has wandered away from Me, don't be alarmed or surprised. You live in a world that has been rigged to distract you. Each time you plow your way through the massive distractions to communicate with Me, you achieve a victory. Rejoice in these tiny triumphs, and they will increasingly light up your days.

*Who will bring any charge against those whom God has chosen?*
*It is God who justifies. Who is he that condemns? Christ*
*Jesus, who died—more than that, who was raised to life—is*
*at the right hand of God and is also interceding for us.*

ROMANS 8:33–34

*Also read:*

HEBREWS 4:14–16

# Empowerment

# Walk Boldly

WALK BY FAITH, NOT BY SIGHT. As you take steps of faith, depending on Me, I will show you how much I can do for you. If you live your life too safely, you will never know the thrill of seeing Me work through you. When I gave you My Spirit, I empowered you to live beyond your natural ability and strength. That's why it is so wrong to measure your energy level against the challenges ahead of you. The issue is not your strength but Mine, which is limitless. By walking close to Me, you can accomplish My purposes in My strength.

*For we walk by faith, not by sight.*

**2 Corinthians 5:7 nkjv**

*Also read:*

**Galatians 5:25; Psalm 59:16–17**

KEEP YOUR EYES ON ME, not only for direction but also for empowerment. I never lead you to do something without equipping you for the task. That is why it's so important to seek My will in everything you do. There are many burned-out Christians who think more is always better, who deem it unspiritual to say no.

In order to know My will, you must spend time with Me—enjoying My Presence. This is not an onerous task but a delightful privilege. I will show you *the path of Life; in My Presence is fullness of Joy; at My right hand there are pleasures forevermore.*

> *But my eyes are fixed on you, O Sovereign LORD; in*
> *you I take refuge—do not give me over to death.*

**PSALM 141:8**

*Also read:*

**ISAIAH 48:17; PSALM 16:11 NKJV**

AS YOU GET OUT OF BED in the morning, be aware of My Presence with you. You may not be thinking clearly yet, but I am. Your early morning thoughts tend to be anxious ones until you get connected with Me. Invite Me into your thoughts by whispering My Name. Suddenly your day brightens and feels more user-friendly. You cannot dread a day that is vibrant with My Presence.

You gain confidence through knowing that I am with you—that you face nothing alone. Anxiety stems from asking the wrong question: "If such and such happens, can I handle it?" The true question is not whether you can cope with whatever happens, but whether you and I together can handle anything that occurs. It is this you-and-I-together factor that gives you confidence to face the day cheerfully.

> *In the morning, O LORD, you hear my voice; in the morning*
> *I lay my requests before you and wait in expectation.*

PSALM 5:3

*Also read:*

PSALM 63:1 NKJV; PHILIPPIANS 4:13

I AM THE CREATOR OF HEAVEN AND EARTH: Lord of all that is and all that will ever be. Although I am unimaginably vast, I choose to dwell within you, permeating you with My Presence. Only in the spirit realm could Someone so infinitely great live within someone so very small. Be awed by the Power and the Glory of My Spirit within you!

Though the Holy Spirit is infinite, *He deigns to be your Helper.* He is always ready to offer assistance; all you need to do is ask. When the path before you looks easy and straight-forward, you may be tempted to go it alone instead of relying on Me. This is when you are in the greatest danger of stumbling. Ask My Spirit to help you as you go each step of the way. Never neglect this glorious Source of strength within you.

> *"And I will pray the Father, and He will give you another Helper, that He may abide with you forever—the Spirit of truth, whom the world cannot receive, because it neither sees Him nor knows Him; but you know Him, for He dwells with you and will be in you."*
>
> JOHN 14:16–17 NKJV

*Also read:*

JOHN 16:7; ZECHARIAH 4:6

# A Yielded Heart

GROW STRONG IN THE LIGHT OF MY PRESENCE. Your weakness does not repel Me. On the contrary, it attracts My Power, which is always available to flow into a yielded heart. Do not condemn yourself for your constant need of help. Instead, come to Me with your gaping neediness; let the Light of My Love fill you.

A yielded heart does not whine or rebel when the going gets rough. It musters the courage to thank Me even during hard times. Yielding yourself to My will is ultimately an act of trust. *In quietness and trust is your strength.*

> *The LORD is gracious and righteous; our God is full of compassion. The LORD protects the simplehearted; when I was in great need, he saved me. Be at rest once more, O my soul, for the LORD has been good to you.*

PSALM 116:5–7

*Also read:*

EPHESIANS 5:20; ISAIAH 30:15

DO NOT LET ANY SET OF CIRCUMSTANCES intimidate you. The more challenging your day, the more of My Power I place at your disposal. You seem to think that I empower you equally each day, but this is not so. Your tendency upon awakening is to assess the difficulties ahead of you, measuring them against your average strength. This is an exercise in unreality.

I know what each of your days will contain, and I empower you accordingly. The degree to which I strengthen you on a given day is based mainly on two variables: the difficulty of your circumstances, and your willingness to depend on Me for help. Try to view challenging days as opportunities to receive more of My Power than usual. Look to Me for all that you need, and watch to see what I will do. *As your day, so shall your strength be.*

*I pray also that the eyes of your heart may be enlightened in order
that you may know the hope to which he has called you, the riches
of his glorious inheritance in the saints, and his incomparably great
power for us who believe. That power is like the working of his mighty
strength, which he exerted in Christ when he raised him from the
dead and seated him at his right hand in the heavenly realms.*

EPHESIANS 1:18–20

*Also read:*

PSALM 105:4; DEUTERONOMY 33:25 NKJV

# Feelings

BE ON GUARD AGAINST THE PIT OF SELF-PITY. When you are weary or unwell, this demonic trap is the greatest danger you face. Don't even go near the edge of the pit. Its edges crumble easily, and before you know it, you are on the way down. It is ever so much harder to get out of the pit than to keep a safe distance from it. That is why I tell you to be on guard.

There are several ways to protect yourself from self-pity. When you are occupied with praising and thanking Me, it is impossible to feel sorry for yourself. Also, the closer you live to Me, the more distance there is between you and the pit. Live in the Light of My Presence by *fixing your eyes on Me*. Then you will be able *to run with endurance the race that is set before you*, without stumbling or falling.

> *Blessed are those who have learned to acclaim you,*
> *who walk in the light of your presence, O LORD.*
>
> PSALM 89:15

> *Also read:*
>
> HEBREWS 12:1–2 NASB

# When You Feel Far from God

I *AM WITH YOU AND FOR YOU*, your constant Companion and Provider. The question is whether you are with Me and for Me. Though I never leave you, you can essentially "leave" Me by ignoring Me: thinking or acting as if I am not with you. When you feel distance in our relationship, you know where the problem lies. My Love for you is constant; *I am the same yesterday, today, and forever.* It is you who change like shifting sand, letting circumstances toss you this way and that.

When you feel far from Me, whisper My Name. This simple act, done in childlike faith, opens your heart to My Presence. Speak to Me in love-tones; prepare to receive My Love, which flows eternally from the cross. I am delighted when you open yourself to My loving Presence.

> *"I am with you and will watch over you wherever you*
> *go, and I will bring you back to this land. I will not leave*
> *you until I have done what I have promised you."*

**GENESIS 28:15**

*Also read:*

**ROMANS 8:31; HEBREWS 13:8; COLOSSIANS 3:17 NKJV**

I WANT YOU TO KNOW HOW SAFE AND SECURE you are in My Presence. That is a fact, totally independent of your feelings. You are on your way to heaven; nothing can prevent you from reaching that destination. There you will see Me face-to-Face, and your Joy will be off the charts by any earthly standards. Even now, you are never separated from Me, though you must see Me through eyes of faith. I will walk with you till the end of time and onward into eternity.

Although My Presence is a guaranteed promise, that does not necessarily change your feelings. When you forget I am with you, you may experience loneliness or fear. It is through awareness of My Presence that Peace displaces negative feelings. Practice the discipline of walking consciously with Me through each day.

*"I give them eternal life, and they shall never perish; no one can snatch them out of my hand. My Father, who has given them to me, is greater than all; no one can snatch them out of my Father's hand."*

JOHN 10:28–29

*Also read:*

1 CORINTHIANS 13:12; PSALM 29:11

# Rays of Hope

SELF-PITY IS A SLIMY, BOTTOMLESS PIT. Once you fall in, you tend to go deeper and deeper into the mire. As you slide down those slippery walls, you are well on your way to depression, and the darkness is profound.

Your only hope is to look up and see the Light of My Presence shining down on you. Though the Light looks dim from your perspective, deep in the pit, those rays of hope can reach you at any depth. While you focus on Me in trust, you rise ever so slowly out of the abyss of despair. Finally, you can reach up and grasp My hand. I will pull you out into the Light again. I will gently cleanse you, washing off the clinging mire. I will cover you with My righteousness and walk with you down the path of Life.

> *He lifted me out of the slimy pit, out of the mud and mire; he*
> *set my feet on a rock and gave me a firm place to stand. He*
> *put a new song in my mouth, a hymn of praise to our God.*
> *Many will see and fear and put their trust in the LORD.*

PSALM 40:2–3

*Also read:*

PSALM 42:5 NASB; PSALM 147:11

BRING ME ALL YOUR FEELINGS, even the ones you wish you didn't have. Fear and anxiety still plague you. Feelings per se are not sinful, but they can be temptations to sin. Blazing missiles of fear fly at you day and night; these attacks from the evil one come at you relentlessly. Use your *shield of faith to extinguish those flaming arrows*. Affirm your trust in Me, regardless of how you feel. If you persist, your feelings will eventually fall in line with your faith.

Do not hide from your fear or pretend it isn't there. Anxiety that you hide in the recesses of your heart will give birth to fear of fear: a monstrous mutation. Bring your anxieties out into the Light of My Presence, where we can deal with them together. Concentrate on trusting Me, and fearfulness will gradually lose its foothold within you.

*In addition to all this, take up the shield of faith, with which you can extinguish all the flaming arrows of the evil one.*

**EPHESIANS 6:16**

*Also read:*

1 JOHN 1:5–7; ISAIAH 12:2

# Love Never Changes

I LOVE YOU WITH AN EVERLASTING LOVE. The human mind cannot comprehend My constancy. Your emotions flicker and falter in the face of varying circumstances, and you tend to project your fickle feelings onto Me. Thus you do not benefit fully from My unfailing Love.

You need to look beyond the flux of circumstances and discover Me gazing lovingly back at you. This awareness of My Presence strengthens you as you receive and respond to My Love. *I am the same yesterday, today, and forever!* Let My Love flow into you continually. Your need for Me is as constant as the out-flow of My Love to you.

> *The LORD appeared to us in the past, saying: "I have loved you with an everlasting love; I have drawn you with loving-kindness."*

**JEREMIAH 31:3**

*Also read:*

**EXODUS 15:13; HEBREWS 13:8**

# Future Concerns

# One Step at a Time

FOLLOW ME ONE STEP AT A TIME. That is all I require of you. In fact, that is the only way to move through this space/time world. You see huge mountains looming, and you start wondering how you're going to scale those heights. Meanwhile, because you're not looking where you're going, you stumble on the easy path where I am leading you now. As I help you get back on your feet, you tell Me how worried you are about the cliffs up ahead. But you don't know what will happen today, much less tomorrow. Our path may take an abrupt turn, leading you away from those mountains. There may be an easier way up the mountains than is visible from this distance. If I do lead you up the cliffs, I will equip you thoroughly for that strenuous climb. *I will even give My angels charge over you, to preserve you in all your ways.*

Keep your mind on the present journey, enjoying My Presence. *Walk by faith, not by sight,* trusting Me to open up the way before you.

> *With your help I can advance against a troop;*
> *with my God I can scale a wall.*
>
> PSALM 18:29

*Also read:*

PSALM 91:11–12 AMP; 2 CORINTHIANS 5:7 NKJV

I AM LEADING YOU, step by step, through your life. Hold My hand in trusting dependence, letting Me guide you through this day. Your future looks uncertain and feels flimsy—even precarious. That is how it should be. *Secret things belong to the Lord*, and future things are secret things. When you try to figure out the future, you are grasping at things that are Mine. This, like all forms of worry, is an act of rebellion: doubting My promises to care for you.

Whenever you find yourself worrying about the future, repent and return to Me. I will show you the next step forward, and the one after that, and the one after that. Relax and enjoy the journey in My Presence, trusting Me to open up the way before you as you go.

> *The secret things belong to the LORD our God, but the things revealed belong to us and to our children forever, that we may follow all the words of this law.*

DEUTERONOMY 29:29

*Also read:*

LUKE 12:25–26; PSALM 32:8

# Avoid Excessive Planning

YOU WILL NOT FIND MY PEACE by engaging in excessive planning, attempting to control what will happen to you in the future. That is a commonly practiced form of unbelief. When your mind spins with multiple plans, Peace may sometimes seem to be within your grasp; yet it always eludes you. Just when you think you have prepared for all possibilities, something unexpected pops up and throws things into confusion.

I did not design the human mind to figure out the future. That is beyond your capability. I crafted your mind for continual communication with Me. Bring Me all your needs, your hopes and fears. Commit everything into My care. Turn from the path of planning to the path of Peace.

*Humble yourselves, therefore, under God's mighty hand, that he may lift you up in due time. Cast all your anxiety on him because he cares for you.*

1 PETER 5:6–7

*Also read:*

PROVERBS 16:9; PSALM 37:5 NKJV

I AM PERPETUALLY WITH YOU, taking care of you. That is the most important fact of your existence. I am not limited by time or space; My Presence with you is a forever-promise. You need not fear the future, for I am already there. When you make that quantum leap into eternity, you will find Me awaiting you in heaven. Your future is in My hands; I release it to you day by day, moment by moment. Therefore, *do not worry about tomorrow.*

I want you to live this day abundantly, seeing all there is to see, doing all there is to do. Don't be distracted by future concerns. Leave them to Me! Each day of life is a glorious gift, but so few people know how to live within the confines of today. Much of their energy for abundant living spills over the timeline into tomorrow's worries or past regrets. Their remaining energy is sufficient only for limping through the day, not for living it to the full. I am training you to keep your focus on My Presence in the present. This is how to receive abundant Life, which flows freely from My throne of grace.

> *"Therefore do not worry about tomorrow, for tomorrow will worry about itself. Each day has enough trouble of its own."*
>
> MATTHEW 6:34

*Also read:*

JOHN 10:10; JAMES 4:13–15

# Don't Worry About the Future

SIT QUIETLY WITH ME, letting all your fears and worries bubble up to the surface of your consciousness. There, in the Light of My Presence, the bubbles pop and disappear. However, some fears surface over and over again, especially fear of the future. You tend to project yourself mentally into the next day, week, month, year, decade; and you visualize yourself coping badly in those times. What you are seeing is a false image, because it doesn't include Me. Those gloomy times that you imagine will not come to pass, since My Presence will be with you at all times.

When a future-oriented worry assails you, capture it and disarm it by suffusing the Light of My Presence into that mental image. Say to yourself, "Jesus will be with me then and there. With His help, I can cope!" Then, come home to the present moment, where you can enjoy Peace in My Presence.

*Then Jesus said to his disciples: "Therefore I tell you, do not worry about your life, what you will eat; or about your body, what you will wear. Life is more than food, and the body more than clothes. Consider the ravens: They do not sow or reap, they have no storeroom or barn; yet God feeds them. And how much more valuable you are than birds! Who of you by worrying can add a single hour to his life?*

LUKE 12:22–25

*Also read:*

DEUTERONOMY 31:6; 2 CORINTHIANS 10:5

LEAVE OUTCOMES UP TO ME. Follow Me wherever I lead, without worrying about how it will all turn out. Think of your life as an adventure, with Me as your Guide and Companion. Live in the now, concentrating on staying in step with Me. When our path leads to a cliff, be willing to climb it with My help. When we come to a resting place, take time to be refreshed in My Presence. Enjoy the rhythm of life lived close to Me.

You already know the ultimate destination of your journey: your entrance into heaven. So keep your focus on the path just before you, leaving outcomes up to Me.

> *"When he has brought out all his own, he goes on ahead of them, and his sheep follow him because they know his voice."*
>
> JOHN 10:4

*Also read:*

PSALM 27:13–14; EXODUS 15:13

# God's Presence

APPROACH EACH NEW DAY with desire to find Me. Before you get out of bed, I have already been working to prepare the path that will get you through this day. There are hidden treasures strategically placed along the way. Some of the treasures are trials, designed to shake you free from earth-shackles. Others are blessings that reveal My Presence: sunshine, flowers, birds, friendships, answered prayer. I have not abandoned this sin-wracked world; I am still richly present in it.

Search for deep treasure as you go through this day. You will find Me all along the way.

> *A man's mind plans his way, but the Lord*
> *directs his steps and makes them sure.*
>
> PROVERBS 16:9 AMP

*Also read:*

COLOSSIANS 2:2–3; ISAIAH 33:6

# Dealing with Uncertainty

REST WITH ME A WHILE. You have journeyed up a steep, rugged path in recent days. The way ahead is shrouded in uncertainty. Look neither behind you nor before you. Instead, focus your attention on Me, your constant Companion. Trust that I will equip you fully for whatever awaits you on your journey.

I designed time to be a protection for you. You couldn't bear to see all your life at once. Though I am unlimited by time, it is in the present moment that I meet you. Refresh yourself in My company, breathing deep draughts of My Presence. The highest level of trust is to enjoy Me moment by moment. *I am with you, watching over you wherever you go.*

> *"Come to Me, all you who labor and are heavy laden, and I will give you rest."*
>
> MATTHEW 11:28 NKJV

*Also read:*

PSALM 143:8; GENESIS 28:15

I AM YOUR BEST FRIEND, as well as your King. Walk hand in hand with Me through your life. Together we will face whatever each day brings: pleasures, hardships, adventures, disappointments. Nothing is wasted when it is shared with Me. *I can bring beauty out of the ashes* of lost dreams. I can glean Joy out of sorrow, Peace out of adversity. Only a Friend who is also the King of kings could accomplish this divine alchemy. There is no other like Me!

The friendship I offer you is practical and down-to-earth, yet it is saturated with heavenly Glory. Living in My Presence means living in two realms simultaneously: the visible world and unseen, eternal reality. I have equipped you to stay conscious of Me while walking along dusty, earthbound paths.

> *"Greater love has no one than this, that he lay down his life for his friends. You are my friends if you do what I command. I no longer call you servants, because a servant does not know his master's business. Instead, I have called you friends, for everything that I learned from my Father I have made known to you."*
>
> JOHN 15:13–15

*Also read:*

ISAIAH 61:3; 2 CORINTHIANS 6:10

# With You Always

I AM ALWAYS AVAILABLE TO YOU. Once you have trusted Me as your Savior, I never distance Myself from you. Sometimes you may *feel* distant from Me. Recognize that as feeling; do not confuse it with reality. The Bible is full of My promises to be with you always. As I assured Jacob, when he was journeying away from home into unknown places, *I am with you and will watch over you wherever you go.* After My resurrection, I made this promise to My followers: *Surely I am with you always, to the very end of the age.* Let these assurances of My continual Presence fill you with Joy and Peace. No matter what you may lose in this life, you can never lose your relationship with Me.

> *"Though the mountains be shaken and the hills be removed, yet my unfailing love for you will not be shaken nor my covenant of peace be removed," says the LORD, who has compassion on you.*
>
> ISAIAH 54:10

*Also read:*

GENESIS 28:15; MATTHEW 28:19–20

REST IN ME, MY CHILD. This time devoted to Me is meant to be peaceful, not stressful. You don't have to perform in order to receive My Love. I have boundless, unconditional Love for you. How it grieves Me to see My children working for Love: trying harder and harder, yet never feeling good enough to be loved.

Be careful that your devotion to Me does not become another form of works. I want you to come into My Presence joyfully and confidently. You have nothing to fear, for you wear My own righteousness. Gaze into My eyes, and you will see no condemnation, only Love and delight in the one I see. Be blessed as *My Face shines radiantly upon you, giving you Peace.*

*"Greater love has no one than this, that he lay down his life for his friends."*

JOHN 15:13

*Also read:*

2 CORINTHIANS 5:21 NKJV; ZEPHANIAH 3:17;
NUMBERS 6:25–26

# Abundant Peace

LIVE FIRST AND FOREMOST in My Presence. Gradually you will become more aware of Me than of people and places around you. This awareness will not detract from your relationships with others. Instead, it will increase your ability to give love and encouragement to them. My Peace will permeate your words and demeanor. You will be active in the world, yet one step removed from it. You will not be easily shaken because My enveloping Presence buffers the blow of problems.

This is the path I have set before you. As you follow it wholeheartedly, you experience abundant Life and Peace.

*Blessed are those who have learned to acclaim you, who walk in the light of your presence, O LORD. They rejoice in your name all day long; they exult in your righteousness.*

PSALM 89:15–16

*Also read:*

PSALM 16:8; 2 PETER 1:2; JOHN 10:28 NKJV

NEVER TAKE FOR GRANTED My intimate nearness. Marvel at the wonder of My continual Presence with you. Even the most ardent human lover cannot be with you always. Nor can another person know the intimacies of your heart, mind, and spirit. *I know everything about you—even the number of hairs on your head.* You don't need to work at revealing yourself to Me.

Many people spend a lifetime or a small fortune searching for someone who understands them. Yet I am freely available to all who call upon My Name, who open their hearts to receive Me as Savior. This simple act of faith is the beginning of a lifelong love story. I, the Lover of your soul, understand you perfectly and love you eternally.

> *The LORD is near to all who call upon Him,*
> *to all who call upon Him in truth.*
>
> PSALM 145:18 NKJV

*Also read:*

LUKE 12:7; JOHN 1:12; ROMANS 10:13

# Stay Conscious of Me

**TRY TO STAY CONSCIOUS OF ME** as you go step by step through this day. My Presence with you is both a promise and a protection. After My resurrection, I assured My followers: *Surely I am with you always.* That promise was for all of My followers, without exception.

The promise of My Presence is a powerful protection. As you journey through your life, there are numerous pitfalls along the way. Many voices clamor for your attention, enticing you to go their way. A few steps away from your true path are pits of self-pity and despair, plateaus of pride and self-will. If you take your eyes off Me and follow another's way, you are in grave danger. Even well-meaning friends can lead you astray if you let them usurp My place in your life. The way to stay on the path of Life is to keep your focus on Me. Awareness of My Presence is your best protection.

> *"And teaching them to obey everything I have commanded you.*
> *And surely I am with you always, to the very end of the age."*
>
> **MATTHEW 28:20**
>
> *Also read:*
>
> **HEBREWS 12:1–2**

*LIE DOWN IN GREEN PASTURES* of Peace. Learn to unwind whenever possible, resting in the Presence of your Shepherd. This electronic age keeps My children "wired" much of the time, too tense to find Me in the midst of their moments. I built into your very being the need for rest. How twisted the world has become when people feel guilty about meeting this basic need! How much time and energy they waste by being always on the go rather than taking time to seek My direction for their lives.

I have called you to walk with Me down *paths of Peace*. I want you to blaze a trail for others who desire to live in My peaceful Presence. I have chosen you less for your strengths than for your weaknesses, which amplify your need for Me. Depend on Me more and more, and I will shower Peace on all your paths.

*The Lord is my shepherd, I shall not be in want. He makes me lie down in green pastures, he leads me beside quiet waters, he restores my soul. He guides me in paths of righteousness for his name's sake.*

PSALM 23:1–3

*Also read:*

GENESIS 2:2–3; LUKE 1:79

# Choose the Scenic Route

*I AM THE PRINCE OF PEACE.* As I said to My disciples, I say also to you: *Peace be with you.* Since I am your constant Companion, My Peace is steadfastly with you. When you keep your focus on Me, you experience both My Presence and My Peace. Worship Me as King of kings, Lord of lords, and Prince of Peace.

You need My Peace each moment to accomplish My purposes in your life. Sometimes you are tempted to take shortcuts in order to reach your goal as quickly as possible. But if the shortcut requires turning your back on My peaceful Presence, you must choose the longer route. Walk with Me along paths of Peace; enjoy the journey in My Presence.

> *For to us a child is born, to us a son is given, and the government*
> *will be on his shoulders. And he will be called Wonderful*
> *Counselor, Mighty God, Everlasting Father, Prince of Peace.*
>
> ISAIAH 9:6
>
> *Also read:*
>
> JOHN 20:19–21; PSALM 25:4 NKJV

LET MY PRESENCE OVERRIDE EVERYTHING you experience. Like a luminous veil of Light, I hover over you and everything around you. I am training you to stay conscious of Me in each situation you encounter.

When the patriarch Jacob ran away from his enraged brother, he went to sleep on a stone pillow in a land that seemed desolate. But after dreaming about heaven and angels and promises of My Presence, he awoke and exclaimed: "Surely the LORD is in this place, and I was not aware of it." His discovery was not only for him but for all who seek Me. Whenever you feel distant from Me, say, "Surely the Lord is in this place!" Then ask Me to give you awareness of My Presence. This is a prayer that I delight to answer.

*In the shelter of your presence you hide them from the intrigues of men; in your dwelling you keep them safe from accusing tongues.*

PSALM 31:20

*Also read:*

GENESIS 28:11–16

# Growth

*I AM THE POTTER; you are My clay.* I designed you before the foundation of the world. I arrange the events of each day to form you into this preconceived pattern. My everlasting Love is at work in every event of your life. On some days your will and Mine flow smoothly together. You tend to feel in control of your life when our wills are in harmony. On other days you feel as if you are swimming upstream, against the current of My purposes. When that happens, stop and seek My Face. The opposition you feel may be from Me, or it may be from the evil one.

Talk with Me about what you are experiencing. Let My Spirit guide you through treacherous waters. As you move through the turbulent stream with Me, let circumstances mold you into the one I desire you to be. Say *yes* to your Potter as you go through this day.

> *Yet, O LORD, you are Father. We are the clay, you are the potter; we are all the work of your hand.*
>
> ISAIAH 64:8

*Also read:*

PSALM 27:8; 1 JOHN 5:5–6 NKJV

# Healing from Brokenness

*I AM A GOD WHO HEALS.* I heal broken bodies, broken minds, broken hearts, broken lives, and broken relationships. My very Presence has immense healing powers. You cannot live close to Me without experiencing some degree of healing. However, it is also true that *you have not because you ask not.* You receive the healing that flows naturally from My Presence, whether you seek it or not. But there is more—much more— available to those who ask.

The first step in receiving healing is to live ever so close to Me. The benefits of this practice are too numerous to list. As you grow more and more intimate with Me, I reveal My will to you more directly. When the time is right, I prompt you to ask for healing of some brokenness in you or in another person. The healing may be instantaneous, or it may be a process. That is up to Me. Your part is to trust Me fully and to thank Me for the restoration that has begun.

I rarely heal all the brokenness in a person's life. Even My servant Paul was told, *"My grace is sufficient for you,"* when he sought healing for the *thorn in his flesh.* Nonetheless, much healing is available to those whose lives are intimately interwoven with Mine. *Ask, and you will receive.*

*Ye have not, because ye ask not.*

**JAMES 4:2 KJV**

*Also read:*

**2 CORINTHIANS 12:7–9; MATTHEW 7:7**

# Identity

COME TO ME FOR UNDERSTANDING since I know you far better than you know yourself. I comprehend you in all your complexity; *no detail of your life is hidden from Me.* I view you through eyes of grace, so don't be afraid of My intimate awareness. Allow the Light of My healing Presence to shine into the deepest recesses of your being—cleansing, healing, refreshing, and renewing you. Trust Me enough to accept the full forgiveness that I offer you continually. This great gift, which cost Me My Life, is yours for all eternity. Forgiveness is at the very core of My abiding Presence. *I will never leave you or forsake you.*

When no one else seems to understand you, simply draw closer to Me. Rejoice in the One who understands you completely and loves you perfectly. As I fill you with My Love, you become a reservoir of love, overflowing into the lives of other people.

> *O Lord, you have searched me and you know me. You know when I sit and when I rise; you perceive my thoughts from afar. You discern my going out and my lying down; you are familiar with all my ways. Before a word is on my tongue you know it completely, O Lord.*

PSALM 139:1–4

*Also read:*

2 CORINTHIANS 1:21–22; JOSHUA 1:5

SEEK MY FACE, and you will find all that you have longed for. The deepest yearnings of your heart are for intimacy with Me. I know because I designed you to desire Me. Do not feel guilty about taking time to be still in My Presence. You are simply responding to the tugs of divinity within you. I made you in My image, and I hid heaven in your heart. Your yearning for Me is a form of homesickness: longing for your true home in heaven.

Do not be afraid to be different from other people. The path I have called you to travel is exquisitely right for you. The more closely you follow My leading, the more fully I can develop your gifts. To follow Me wholeheartedly, you must relinquish your desire to please other people. However, your closeness to Me will bless others by enabling you to shine brightly in this dark world.

*As the deer pants for streams of water, so my soul pants for you, O God. My soul thirsts for God, for the living God. When can I go and meet with God?*

PSALM 42:1–2

*Also read:*

PSALM 34:5; PHILIPPIANS 2:15

# Live in Union with Me

I DESIGNED YOU to live in union with Me. This union does not negate who you are; it actually makes you more fully yourself. When you try to live independently of Me, you experience emptiness and dissatisfaction. You may *gain the whole world* and yet lose everything that really counts.

Find fulfillment through living close to Me, yielding to My purposes for you. Though I may lead you along paths that feel alien to you, trust that I know what I am doing. If you follow Me wholeheartedly, you will discover facets of yourself that were previously hidden. I know you intimately—far better than you know yourself. In union with Me, you are complete. In closeness to Me, you are transformed more and more into the one I designed you to be.

> *"What good is it for a man to gain the*
> *whole world, yet forfeit his soul?"*
>
> MARK 8:36

*Also Read:*

PSALM 139:13–16; 2 CORINTHIANS 3:17–18

# Making Mistakes

# Release Your Mistakes

DON'T BE SO HARD ON YOURSELF. I can bring good even out of your mistakes. Your finite mind tends to look backward, longing to undo decisions you have come to regret. This is a waste of time and energy, leading only to frustration. Instead of floundering in the past, release your mistakes to Me. Look to Me in trust, anticipating that My infinite creativity can weave both good choices and bad into a lovely design.

Because you are human, you will continue to make mistakes. Thinking that you should live an error-free life is symptomatic of pride. Your failures can be a source of blessing, humbling you and giving you empathy for other people in their weaknesses. Best of all, failure highlights your dependence on Me. I am able to bring beauty out of the morass of your mistakes. Trust Me, and watch to see what I will do.

*And we know that in all things God works for the good of those who love him, who have been called according to his purpose.*

ROMANS 8:28

*Also read:*

PROVERBS 11:2; MICAH 7:7

**WHEN YOUR SINS WEIGH HEAVILY** upon you, come to Me. Confess your wrongdoing, which I know all about before you say a word. Stay in the Light of My Presence, receiving forgiveness, cleansing, and healing. Remember that *I have clothed you in My righteousness*, so nothing can separate you from Me. Whenever you stumble or fall, I am there to help you up.

Man's tendency is to hide from his sin, seeking refuge in the darkness. There he indulges in self-pity, denial, self-righteousness, blaming, and hatred. But *I am the Light of the world*, and My illumination decimates the darkness. Come close to Me and let My Light envelop you, driving out darkness and permeating you with Peace.

> *But if we walk in the light, as he is in the light, we have fellowship with one another, and the blood of Jesus, his Son, purifies us from all sin.*

1 JOHN 1:7

*Also read:*

ISAIAH 61:10; JOHN 8:12

# Unconditional Love

I AM THE GIFT THAT CONTINUOUSLY GIVES —bounteously, with no strings attached. Unconditional Love is such a radical concept that even My most devoted followers fail to grasp it fully. Absolutely nothing in heaven or on earth can cause Me to stop loving you. You may *feel* more loved when you are performing according to your expectations. But My Love for you is perfect; therefore it is not subject to variation. What *does* vary is your awareness of My loving Presence.

When you are dissatisfied with your behavior, you tend to feel unworthy of My Love. You may unconsciously punish yourself by withdrawing from Me and attributing the distance between us to My displeasure. Instead of returning to Me and receiving My Love, you attempt to earn My approval by trying harder. All the while, I am aching to hold you in *My everlasting arms*, to enfold you in My Love. When you are feeling unworthy or unloved, come to Me. Then ask for receptivity to *My unfailing Love*.

> *If anyone acknowledges that Jesus is the Son of God,*
> *God lives in him and he in God. And so we know and*
> *rely on the love God has for us. God is love. Whoever*
> *lives in love lives in God, and God in him.*
>
> 1 JOHN 4:15–16

> *Also read:*
>
> DEUTERONOMY 33:27; PSALM 13:5; 1 JOHN 4:18

# Perspective

# Everything Belongs to Me

LET ME TEACH YOU THANKFULNESS. Begin by acknowledging that everything—all your possessions and all that you are—belongs to Me. The dawning of each new day is a gift from Me, not to be taken for granted. The earth is vibrantly alive with My blessings, giving vivid testimony to My Presence. If you slow down your pace of life, you can find Me anywhere.

Some of My most precious children have been laid aside in sickbeds or shut away in prisons. Others have voluntarily learned the discipline of spending time alone with Me. The secret of being thankful is learning to see everything from My perspective. My world is your classroom. *My Word is a lamp to your feet and a light for your path.*

> *Therefore, since we are receiving a kingdom that cannot be shaken, let us be thankful, and so worship God acceptably with reverence and awe, for our "God is a consuming fire."*
>
> HEBREWS 12:28–29

*Also read:*

PSALM 19:1 NKJV; PSALM 119:105

**LEARN TO LAUGH AT YOURSELF** more freely. Don't take yourself or your circumstances so seriously. Relax and know that I am *God with you*. When you desire My will above all else, life becomes much less threatening. Stop trying to monitor My responsibilities—things that are beyond your control. Find freedom by accepting the boundaries of your domain.

Laughter lightens your load and lifts your heart into heavenly places. Your laughter rises to heaven and blends with angelic melodies of praise. Just as parents delight in the laughter of their children, so I delight in hearing My children laugh. I rejoice when you trust Me enough to enjoy your life lightheartedly.

Do not miss the Joy of My Presence by carrying the weight of the world on your shoulders. Rather, *take My yoke upon you and learn from Me. My yoke is comfortable and pleasant; My burden is light and easily borne.*

> *A cheerful heart is good medicine, but a*
> *crushed spirit dies up the bones.*
>
> PROVERBS 17:22

*Also read:*

PROVERBS 31:25; MATTHEW 1:23;
MATTHEW 11:29–30 AMP

# Trust in the Midst

TRUST ME IN THE MIDST of a messy day. Your inner calm—your Peace in My Presence—need not be shaken by what is going on around you. Though you live in this temporal world, your innermost being is rooted and grounded in eternity. When you start to feel stressed, detach yourself from the disturbances around you. Instead of desperately striving to maintain order and control in your little world, relax and remember that circumstances cannot touch My Peace.

Seek My Face, and I will share My mind with you, opening your eyes to see things from My perspective. *Do not let your heart be troubled, and do not be afraid.* The Peace I give is sufficient for you.

> *"I have told you these things, so that in me you may*
> *have peace. In this world you will have trouble. But*
> *take heart! I have overcome the world."*
>
> JOHN 16:33

> *Also read:*
>
> PSALM 105:4; JOHN 14:27

# Let Go of Worry

TRY TO SEE THINGS more and more from My perspective. Let the Light of My Presence so fully fill your mind that you view the world through Me. When little things don't go as you had hoped, look to Me lightheartedly and say, "Oh, well." This simple discipline can protect you from being burdened with an accumulation of petty cares and frustrations. If you practice this diligently, you will make a life-changing discovery: You realize that most of the things that worry you are not important. If you shrug them off immediately and return your focus to Me, you will walk through your days with lighter steps and a joyful heart.

When serious problems come your way, you will have more reserves for dealing with them. You will not have squandered your energy on petty problems. You may even reach the point where you can agree with the apostle Paul that all your troubles are *light and momentary* compared with *the eternal glory* being achieved by them.

*For with You is the fountain of life; in Your light we see light.*

PSALM 36:9 NKJV

*Also read:*

PROVERBS 20:24; 2 CORINTHIANS 4:17–18

# The One Thing You Can't Lose

I AM THE CULMINATION of all your hopes and desires. *I am the Alpha and the Omega, the first and the last: who is and was and is to come.* Before you knew Me, you expressed your longing for Me in hurtful ways. You were ever so vulnerable to the evil around you in the world. But now My Presence safely shields you, enfolding you in My loving arms. *I have lifted you out of darkness into My marvelous Light.*

Though I have brought many pleasures into your life, not one of them is essential. Receive My blessings with open hands. Enjoy My good gifts, but do not cling to them. Turn your attention to the *Giver of all good things*, and rest in the knowledge that you are complete in Me. The one thing you absolutely need is the one thing you can never lose: My Presence with you.

*Find rest, O my soul, in God alone; my hope comes from him.*
*He alone is my rock and my salvation; he is my fortress, I will*
*not be shaken. My salvation and my honor depend on God;*
*he is my mighty rock, my refuge. Trust in him at all times, O*
*people; pour out your hearts to him, for God is our refuge.*

PSALM 62:5–8

*Also read:*

REVELATION 1:8; 1 PETER 2:9 NKJV; JAMES 1:17

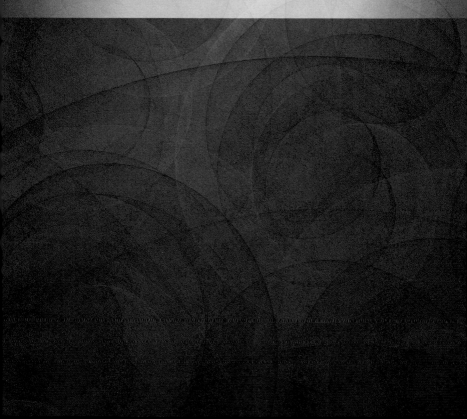

# Prayer

# Your Greatest Strength

YOU NEED ME EVERY MOMENT. Your awareness of your constant need for Me is your greatest strength. Your neediness, properly handled, is a link to My Presence. However, there are pitfalls that you must be on guard against: self-pity, self-preoccupation, giving up. Your inadequacy presents you with a continual choice—deep dependence on Me or despair. The emptiness you feel within will be filled either with problems or with My Presence. Make Me central in your consciousness by *praying continually*: simple, short prayers flowing out of the present moment. Use My Name liberally, to remind you of My Presence. *Keep on asking and you will receive, so that your gladness may be full and complete.*

*In the day of my trouble I will call*
*to you, for you will answer me.*

PSALM 86:7

*Also read:*

1 THESSALONIANS 5:17; JOHN 16:24 AMP

I AM CALLING YOU to a life of constant communion with Me. Basic training includes learning to live above your circumstances, even while interacting on that cluttered plane of life. You yearn for a simplified lifestyle so that your communication with Me can be uninterrupted. But I challenge you to relinquish the fantasy of an uncluttered world. Accept each day just as it comes, and find Me in the midst of it all.

Talk with Me about every aspect of your day, including your feelings. Remember that your ultimate goal is not to control or fix everything around you; it is to keep communing with Me. A successful day is one in which you have stayed in touch with Me, even if many things remain undone at the end of the day. Do not let your to-do list (written or mental) become an idol directing your life. Instead, ask My Spirit to guide you moment by moment. He will keep you close to Me.

*Pray continually.*

1 THESSALONIANS 5:17

*Also read:*

PROVERBS 3:6; GALATIANS 5:25

# Molding Your Mind

FOCUS YOUR ENTIRE BEING on My living Presence. I am most assuredly with you, enveloping you in My Love and Peace. While you relax in My Presence, I am molding your mind and cleansing your heart. I am re-creating you into the one I designed you to be.

As you move from stillness into the activities of your day, do not relinquish your attentiveness to Me. If something troubles you, talk it over with Me. If you get bored with what you are doing, fill the time with prayers and praise. When someone irritates you, don't let your thoughts linger on that person's faults. Gently nudge your mind back to Me. Every moment is precious if you keep your focus on Me. Any day can be a good day because My Presence permeates all time.

*Blessed are those who have learned to acclaim you, who walk in the light of your presence, O LORD. They rejoice in your name all day long; they exult in your righteousness.*

PSALM 89:15–16

*Also read:*

1 JOHN 3:19–20; JUDE vv.24–25; PSALM 41:12

# Relating to Others

# Serve Only One Master

*YOU CANNOT SERVE TWO MASTERS.* If I am truly your Master, you will desire to please Me above all others. If pleasing people is your goal, you will be enslaved to them. People can be harsh taskmasters when you give them this power over you.

If I am the Master of your life, I will also be your *First Love*. Your serving Me is rooted and grounded in My vast, unconditional Love for you. The lower you bow down before Me, the higher I lift you up into intimate relationship with Me. *The Joy of living in My Presence* outshines all other pleasures. I want you to reflect My joyous Light by living in increasing intimacy with Me.

> *"No one can serve two masters. Either he will hate the one and love the other, or he will be devoted to the one and despise the other. You cannot serve both God and Money."*

MATTHEW 6:24

*Also read:*

REVELATION 2:4; EPHESIANS 3:16–17; PSALM 16:11

LEARN TO RELATE TO OTHERS through My Love rather than yours. Your human love is ever so limited, full of flaws and manipulation. My loving Presence, which always enfolds you, is available to bless others as well as you. Instead of trying harder to help people through your own paltry supplies, become aware of My unlimited supply, which is accessible to you continually. Let My Love envelop your outreach to other people.

Many of My precious children have fallen prey to burnout. A better description of their condition might be "drainout." Countless interactions with needy people have drained them, without their conscious awareness. You are among these weary ones, who are like wounded soldiers needing R & R. Take time to rest in the Love-Light of My Presence. I will gradually restore to you the energy that you have lost over the years. *Come to Me, all you who are weary and burdened, and you will find rest for your souls.*

*Your love, O Lord, reaches to the heavens,*
*your faithfulness to the skies.*

PSALM 36:5

*Also read:*

EXODUS 33:14; MATTHEW 11:28–29

# My Love Covers Sins

**SEEK TO LIVE IN MY LOVE,** which *covers a multitude of sins*: both yours and others'. Wear My Love like a cloak of Light, covering you from head to toe. Have no fear, for *perfect Love decimates fear*. Look at other people through lenses of Love; see them from My perspective. This is how you walk in the Light, and it pleases Me.

I want My body of believers to be radiant with the Light of My Presence. How I grieve when pockets of darkness increasingly dim the Love-Light. Return to Me, your *First Love*! Gaze at Me in the splendor of holiness, and My Love will once again envelop you in Light.

> *Above all, love each other deeply, because*
> *love covers over a multitude of sins.*
>
> **1 PETER 4:8**

*Also read:*

**1 JOHN 4:18; REVELATION 2:4**

WATCH YOUR WORDS DILIGENTLY. Words have such great power to bless or to wound. When you speak carelessly or negatively, you damage others as well as yourself. This ability to verbalize is an awesome privilege, granted only to those I created in My image. You need help in wielding this mighty power responsibly.

Though the world applauds quick-witted retorts, My instructions about communication are quite different: *Be quick to listen, slow to speak, and slow to become angry.* Ask My Spirit to help you whenever you speak. I have trained you to pray—"Help me, Holy Spirit"—before answering the phone, and you have seen the benefits of this discipline. Simply apply the same discipline to communicating with people around you. If they are silent, pray before speaking to them. If they are talking, pray before responding. These are split-second prayers, but they put you in touch with My Presence. In this way, your speaking comes under the control of My Spirit. As positive speech patterns replace your negative ones, the increase in your Joy will amaze you.

> *Reckless words pierce like a sword, but the*
> *tongue of the wise brings healing.*

PROVERBS 12:18

*Also read:*

JAMES 1:19; EPHESIANS 4:29

# Grow in Grace

DO NOT EXPECT TO BE TREATED FAIRLY in this life. People will say and do hurtful things to you, things that you don't deserve. When someone mistreats you, try to view it as an opportunity to grow in grace. See how quickly you can forgive the one who has wounded you. Don't be concerned about setting the record straight. Instead of obsessing about other people's opinions of you, keep your focus on Me. Ultimately, it is My view of you that counts.

As you concentrate on relating to Me, remember that I have clothed you in My righteousness and holiness. I see you attired in these radiant garments, which I bought for you with My blood. This also is not fair; it is pure gift. When others treat you unfairly, remember that My ways with you are much better than fair. My ways are Peace and *Love, which I have poured out into your heart by My Spirit.*

> *Bear with each other and forgive whatever grievances you may have against one another. Forgive as the Lord forgave you.*
>
> COLOSSIANS 3:13

*Also read:*

ISAIAH 61:10; EPHESIANS 1:7–8; ROMANS 5:5

COME TO ME, and rest in My Peace. My Face is shining upon you, in rays of *Peace transcending understanding*. Instead of trying to figure things out yourself, you can relax in the Presence of the One who knows everything. As you lean on Me in trusting dependence, you feel peaceful and complete. This is how I designed you to live: in close communion with Me.

When you are around other people, you tend to cater to their expectations—real or imagined. You feel enslaved to pleasing them, and your awareness of My Presence grows dim. Your efforts to win their approval eventually exhaust you. You offer these people dry crumbs rather than the *living water* of My Spirit flowing through you. This is not My way for you! Stay in touch with Me, even during your busiest moments. Let My Spirit give you words of grace as you live in the Light of My Peace.

*Do not be anxious about anything, but in everything, by prayer*
*and petition, with thanksgiving, present your requests to God.*
*And the peace of God, which transcends all understanding,*
*will guard your hearts and your minds in Christ Jesus.*

PHILIPPIANS 4:6–7

*Also read:*

JOHN 7:38; EPHESIANS 5:18–20

# Finding Yourself

I AM LEADING YOU along a way that is uniquely right for you. The closer to Me you grow, the more fully you become your true self—the one I designed you to be. Because you are one of a kind, the path you are traveling with Me diverges increasingly from that of other people. However, in My mysterious wisdom and ways, I enable you to follow this solitary path while staying in close contact with others. In fact, the more completely you devote yourself to Me, the more freely you can love people.

Marvel at the beauty of a life intertwined with My Presence. Rejoice as we journey together in intimate communion. Enjoy the adventure of finding yourself through losing yourself in Me.

*Therefore, if anyone is in Christ, he is a new creation; the old has gone, the new has come!*

2 CORINTHIANS 5:17

*Also read:*

EPHESIANS 2:10; 1 JOHN 4:7–8; JOHN 15:4

# Renewing
# Your Mind

# A Teachable Spirit

FROM JANUARY 1

COME TO ME WITH A TEACHABLE SPIRIT, eager to be changed. A close walk with Me is a life of continual newness. Do not cling to old ways as you step into a new year. Instead, seek My Face with an open mind, knowing that your journey with Me involves being *transformed by the renewing of your mind*. As you focus your thoughts on Me, be aware that I am fully attentive to you. I see you with a steady eye because My attention span is infinite. I know and understand you completely; My thoughts embrace you in everlasting Love. *I also know the plans I have for you: plans to prosper you and not to harm you, plans to give you hope and a future.* Give yourself fully to this adventure of increasing attentiveness to My Presence.

*You have said, "Seek my face." My heart says
to you, "Your face, LORD, do I seek."*

PSALM 27:8 ESV

*Also read:*

ROMANS 12:2; JEREMIAH 29:11

**KEEP YOUR FOCUS ON ME.** I have gifted you with amazing freedom, including the ability to choose the focal point of your mind. Only the crown of My creation has such remarkable capability; this is a sign of being *made in My image*.

Let the goal of this day be to *bring every thought captive to Me*. Whenever your mind wanders, lasso those thoughts and bring them into My Presence. In My radiant Light, anxious thoughts shrink and shrivel away. Judgmental thoughts are unmasked as you bask in My unconditional Love. Confused ideas are untangled while you rest in the simplicity of My Peace. *I will guard you and keep you in constant Peace, as you focus your mind on Me.*

> *You made him a little lower than the heavenly beings*
> *and crowned him with glory and honor.*

**PSALM 8:5**

*Also read:*

**GENESIS 1:26–27; 2 CORINTHIANS 10:5; ISAIAH 26:3 AMP**

# Guard Your Thoughts

WORSHIP ME ONLY. Whatever occupies your mind the most becomes your god. Worries, if indulged, develop into idols. Anxiety gains a life of its own, parasitically infesting your mind. Break free from this bondage by affirming your trust in Me and refreshing yourself in My Presence. What goes on in your mind is invisible, undetectable to other people. But I read your thoughts continually, searching for evidence of trust in Me. I rejoice when your mind turns toward Me. Guard your thoughts diligently; good thought-choices will keep you close to Me.

*He will have no fear of bad news; his heart is steadfast, trusting in the LORD.*

PSALM 112:7

*Also read:*

1 CORINTHIANS 13:11; PSALM 139:23–24 NASB

LET ME CONTROL YOUR MIND. The mind is the most restless, unruly part of mankind. Long after you have learned the discipline of holding your tongue, your thoughts defy your will and set themselves up against Me. Man is the pinnacle of My creation, and the human mind is wondrously complex. I risked all by granting you freedom to think for yourself. This is godlike privilege, forever setting you apart from animals and robots. *I made you in My image*, precariously close to deity.

Though My blood has fully redeemed you, your mind is the last bastion of rebellion. Open yourself to My radiant Presence, letting My Light permeate your thinking. *When My Spirit is controlling your mind, you are filled with Life and Peace.*

*The mind controlled by the Spirit is life and peace.*

ROMANS 8:6

*Also read:*

PSALM 8:5 NKJV; GENESIS 1:26–27

# Peace That Surpasses Understanding

THE PEACE THAT I GIVE you transcends your intellect. When most of your mental energy goes into efforts to figure things out, you are unable to receive this glorious gift. I look into your mind and see thoughts spinning round and round: going nowhere, accomplishing nothing. All the while, My Peace hovers over you, searching for a place to land.

Be still in My Presence, inviting Me to control your thoughts. Let My Light soak into your mind and heart until you are aglow with My very Being. This is the most effective way to receive My Peace.

*Now may the Lord of peace himself give you*
*peace at all times and in every way.*

2 THESSALONIANS 3:16

*Also read:*

ZECHARIAH 2:13; JOB 22:21

**TRUST ME IN ALL YOUR THOUGHTS.** I know that some thoughts are unconscious or semiconscious, and I do not hold you responsible for those. But you can direct conscious thoughts much more than you may realize. Practice thinking in certain ways—trusting Me, thanking Me—and those thoughts become more natural. Reject negative or sinful thoughts as soon as you become aware of them. Don't try to hide them from Me; confess them and leave them with Me. Go on your way lightheartedly. This method of controlling your thoughts will keep your mind in My Presence and your feet on the *path of Peace*.

> *Some trust in chariots and some in horses, but we*
> *trust in the name of the LORD our God.*
>
> **PSALM 20:7**

*Also read:*

**1 JOHN 1:9; LUKE 1:79**

# Trust Me, Not Your Own Understanding

*FROM AUGUST 7*

UNDERSTANDING WILL NEVER BRING YOU PEACE. That's why I have instructed you to *trust in Me, not in your understanding.* Human beings have a voracious appetite for trying to figure things out in order to gain a sense of mastery over their lives. But the world presents you with an endless series of problems. As soon as you master one set, another pops up to challenge you. The relief you had anticipated is short-lived. Soon your mind is gearing up again: searching for understanding (mastery) instead of seeking Me (your Master).

The wisest of all men, Solomon, could never think his way through to Peace. His vast understanding resulted in feelings of futility rather than in fulfillment. Finally, he lost his way and succumbed to the will of his wives by worshiping idols.

My Peace is not an elusive goal, hidden at the center of some complicated maze. Actually, you are always enveloped in Peace, which is inherent in My Presence. As you look to Me, you gain awareness of this precious Peace.

> *Trust in the LORD with all your heart and lean not on your own understanding; in all your ways acknowledge him, and he will make your paths straight.*
>
> PROVERBS 3:5–6

*Also read:*

ROMANS 5:1; 2 THESSALONIANS 3:16

THERE IS A MIGHTY BATTLE going on for control of your mind. Heaven and earth intersect in your mind; the tugs of both spheres influence your thinking. I created you with the capacity to experience foretastes of heaven. When you shut out the world and focus on My Presence, you can enjoy sitting with Me *in heavenly realms.* This is an incredible privilege reserved for precious ones who belong to Me and seek My Face. Your greatest strength is your desire to spend time communing with Me. As you concentrate on Me, *My Spirit fills your mind with Life and Peace.*

The world exerts a downward pull on your thoughts. Media bombard you with greed, lust, and cynicism. When you face these things, pray for protection and discernment. Stay in continual communication with Me whenever you walk through the wastelands of this world. Refuse to worry, because this form of worldliness will weigh you down and block awareness of My Presence. Stay alert, recognizing the battle being waged against your mind. Look forward to an eternity of strife-free living, reserved for you in heaven.

*And God raised us up with Christ and seated us with*
*him in the heavenly realms in Christ Jesus.*

EPHESIANS 2:6

*Also read:*

ROMANS 8:6; 1 JOHN 2:15, 17

# Time

SPENDING TIME ALONE WITH ME IS ESSENTIAL for your well-being. It is not a luxury or an option; it is a necessity. Therefore, do not feel guilty about taking time to be with Me. Remember that Satan is *the accuser of believers*. He delights in heaping guilt feelings upon you, especially when you are enjoying My Presence. When you feel Satan's arrows of accusation, you are probably on the right track. Use your *shield of faith* to protect yourself from him. Talk with Me about what you are experiencing, and ask Me to show you the way forward. *Resist the devil, and he will flee from you. Come near to Me, and I will come near to you.*

*Then I heard a loud voice in heaven say: "Now have come the salvation and the power and the kingdom of our God, and the authority of his Christ. For the accuser of our brothers, who accuses them before our God day and night, has been hurled down."*

REVELATION 12:10

*Also read:*

EPHESIANS 6:16; JAMES 4:7–8

# Soak in My Presence

I AM LIFE AND LIGHT IN ABUNDANCE. As you spend time "soaking" in My Presence, you are energized and lightened. Through communing with Me, you transfer your heavy burdens to My strong shoulders. By gazing at Me, you gain My perspective on your life. This time alone with Me is essential for unscrambling your thoughts and smoothing out the day before you.

Be willing to fight for this precious time with Me. Opposition comes in many forms: your own desire to linger in bed; the evil one's determination to distract you from Me; the pressure of family, friends, and your own inner critic to spend your time more productively. As you grow in your desire to please Me above all else, you gain strength to resist these opponents. *Delight yourself in Me, for I am the deepest Desire of your heart.*

*Within your temple, O God, we meditate on your unfailing love.*

PSALM 48:9

*Also read:*

DEUTERONOMY 33:12; PSALM 37:4

**RELAX IN MY HEALING, HOLY PRESENCE.** Allow Me to transform you through this time alone with Me. As your thoughts center more and more on Me, trust displaces fear and worry. Your mind is somewhat like a seesaw. As your trust in Me goes up, fear and worry automatically go down. Time spent with Me not only increases your trust; it also helps you discern what is important and what is not.

Energy and time are precious, limited entities. Therefore, you need to use them wisely, focusing on what is truly important. As you walk close to Me, saturating your mind with Scripture, I will show you how to spend your time and energy. *My Word is a lamp to your feet; My Presence is a Light for your path.*

> *And do not be conformed to this world, but be transformed*
> *by the renewing of your mind, that you may prove what*
> *is that good and acceptable and perfect will of God.*

ROMANS 12:2 NKJV

*Also read:*

PSALM 52:8; EPHESIANS 5:15–16 NKJV; PSALM 119:105

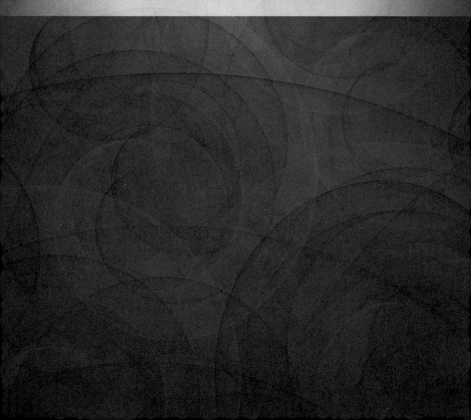

# Trust

STRIVE TO TRUST ME in more and more areas of your life. Anything that tends to make you anxious is a growth opportunity. Instead of running away from these challenges, embrace them, eager to gain all the blessings I have hidden in the difficulties. If you believe that I am sovereign over every aspect of your life, it is possible to trust Me in all situations. Don't waste energy regretting the way things are or thinking about what might have been. Start at the present moment—accepting things exactly as they are—and search for My way in the midst of those circumstances.

Trust is like a staff you can lean on as you journey uphill with Me. If you are trusting in Me consistently, the staff will bear as much of your weight as needed. *Lean on, trust, and be confident in Me with all your heart and mind.*

> *But I am like an olive tree flourishing in the house of God;*
> *I trust in God's unfailing love for ever and ever.*

**PSALM 52:8**

*Also read:*

**PROVERBS 3:5–6 AMP**

# The Pathway of Trust

**TRUST IS A GOLDEN PATHWAY TO HEAVEN.** When you walk on this path, you live above your circumstances. My glorious Light shines more brightly on those who follow this path of Life. Dare to walk on the high road with Me, for it is the most direct route to heaven. The low road is circuitous: twisting and turning in agonizing knots. There the air hangs heavy—and dark, ominous clouds predominate. *Relying on your own understanding* will weigh you down. *Trust in Me absolutely, and I will make your path straight.*

> *"Do not let your hearts be troubled. Trust in God; trust also in me.*
> *In my Father's house are many rooms; if it were not so, I would*
> *have told you. I am going there to prepare a place for you."*
>
> JOHN 14:1–2

*Also read:*

2 TIMOTHY 4:18; PROVERBS 3:5–6

GIVE YOURSELF FULLY to the adventure of today. Walk boldly along the path of Life, relying on your ever-present Companion. You have every reason to be confident because My Presence accompanies you all the days of your life—and onward into eternity.

Do not give in to fear or worry, those robbers of abundant living. Trust Me enough to face problems as they come, rather than trying to anticipate them. *Fix your eyes on Me, the Author and Perfecter of your faith*, and many difficulties on the road ahead will vanish before you reach them. Whenever you start to feel afraid, remember that *I am holding you by your right hand*. Nothing can separate you from My Presence!

> *For this God is our God for ever and ever; he*
> *will be our guide even to the end.*
>
> PSALM 48:14

*Also read:*

HEBREWS 12:2; ISAIAH 41:13

# Your Future Is Assured

YOU ARE MINE FOR ALL TIME—and beyond time, into eternity. No power can deny you your inheritance in heaven. I want you to realize how utterly secure you are! Even if you falter as you journey through life, I will never let go of your hand.

Knowing that your future is absolutely assured can free you to live abundantly today. I have prepared this day for you with the most tender concern and attention to detail. Instead of approaching the day as a blank page that you need to fill up, try living it in a responsive mode, being on the lookout for all that I am doing. This sounds easy, but it requires a deep level of trust, based on the knowledge that *My way is perfect.*

*If the LORD delights in a man's way, he makes his steps firm; though he stumble, he will not fall, for the LORD upholds him with his hand.*

PSALM 37:23–24

*Also read:*

1 PETER 1:3–4; PSALM 18:30

WAITING, TRUSTING, AND HOPING are intricately connected, like golden strands interwoven to form a strong chain. Trusting is the central strand because it is the response from My children that I desire the most. Waiting and hoping embellish the central strand and strengthen the chain that connects you to Me. Waiting for Me to work, with your eyes on Me, is evidence that you really do trust Me. If you mouth the words "I trust You" while anxiously trying to make things go your way, your words ring hollow. Hoping is future-directed, connecting you to your inheritance in heaven. However, the benefits of hope fall fully on you in the present.

Because you are Mine, you don't just pass time in your waiting. You can wait expectantly, in hopeful trust. Keep your "antennae" out to pick up even the faintest glimmer of My Presence.

> *"Do not let your hearts be troubled.*
> *Trust in God; trust also in me."*
>
> **JOHN 14:1**

*Also read:*

**PSALM 27:14; HEBREWS 6:18–20**

# Equipped for Today

FROM MARCH 18

TRUST ME ONE DAY AT A TIME. This keeps you close to Me, responsive to My will. Trust is not a natural response, especially for those who have been deeply wounded. My Spirit within you is your resident Tutor, helping you in this supernatural endeavor. Yield to His gentle touch; be sensitive to His prompting.

Exert your will to trust Me in all circumstances. Don't let your need to understand distract you from My Presence. I will equip you to get through this day victoriously as you live in deep dependence on Me. *Tomorrow is busy worrying about itself; don't get tangled up in its worry-webs.* Trust Me one day at a time.

*O Lord Almighty, blessed is the man who trusts in you.*

PSALM 84:12

*Also read:*

1 CORINTHIANS 6:19; JEREMIAH 17:7 NKJV;
MATTHEW 6:34

REJOICE AND BE THANKFUL! As you walk with Me through this day, practice trusting and thanking Me all along the way. Trust is the channel through which My Peace flows into you. Thankfulness lifts you up above your circumstances.

I do My greatest works through people with grateful, trusting hearts. Rather than planning and evaluating, practice trusting and thanking Me continually. This is a paradigm shift that will revolutionize your life.

*Rejoice in the Lord always. I will say it again: Rejoice!*

PHILIPPIANS 4:4

*Also read:*

PSALM 95:1–2; PSALM 9:10;
2 CORINTHIANS 2:14 NKJV

# A Fork in the Road

TRUSTING ME is a moment-by-moment choice. My people have not always understood this truth. After I performed miracles in the wilderness, My chosen children trusted Me intensely—but only temporarily. Soon the grumbling began again, testing My patience to the utmost.

Isn't it often the same way with you? You trust Me when things go well, when you see Me working on your behalf. This type of trust flows readily within you, requiring no exertion of your will. When things go wrong, your trust-flow slows down and solidifies. You are forced to choose between trusting Me intentionally or rebelling, resenting My ways with you. This choice constitutes a fork in the road. Stay on the path of Life with Me, enjoying My Presence. Choose to trust Me in all circumstances.

*Then Moses led Israel from the Red Sea and they went into the Desert of Shur. For three days they traveled in the desert without finding water. When they came to Marah, they could not drink its water because it was bitter. (That is why the place is called Marah.) So the people grumbled against Moses, saying, "What are we to drink?" Then Moses cried out to the LORD, and the LORD showed him a piece of wood. He threw it into the water, and the water became sweet. There the Lord made a decree and a law for them, and there he tested them.*

EXODUS 15:22–25

*Also read:*

PSALM 31:14

# Let Go of Old Ways

DRAW NEAR TO ME with a thankful heart, aware that your cup is overflowing with blessings. Gratitude enables you to perceive Me more clearly and to rejoice in our Love-relationship. *Nothing can separate you from My loving Presence!* That is the basis of your security. Whenever you start to feel anxious, remind yourself that your security rests in Me alone, and I am totally trustworthy.

You will never be in control of your life circumstances, but you can relax and trust in My control. Instead of striving for a predictable, safe lifestyle, seek to know Me in greater depth and breadth. I long to make your life a glorious adventure, but you must stop clinging to old ways. I am always doing something new within My beloved ones. Be on the lookout for all that I have prepared for you.

*For I am convinced that neither death nor life, neither angels nor demons, neither the present nor the future, now any powers, neither height nor depth, nor anything else in all creation, will be able to separate us from the love of God that is in Christ Jesus our Lord.*

ROMANS 8:38–39

*Also read:*

PSALM 56:3–4; ISAIAH 43:19

# Be Yourself

**RELAX IN MY PEACEFUL PRESENCE.** Do not bring performance pressures into our sacred space of communion. When you are with someone you trust completely, you feel free to be yourself. This is one of the joys of true friendship. Though I am *Lord of lords and King of kings*, I also desire to be your intimate Friend. When you are tense or pretentious in our relationship, I feel hurt. I know the worst about you, but I also see the best in you. I long for you to trust Me enough to be fully yourself with Me. When you are real with Me, I am able to bring out the best in you: the very gifts I have planted in your soul. Relax and enjoy our friendship.

> *Now may the Lord of peace Himself give you peace*
> *always in every way. The Lord be with you all.*
>
> **2 THESSALONIANS 3:16 NKJV**

*Also read:*

**REVELATION 17:14; JOHN 15:13–15**

**WALK WITH ME ALONG PATHS OF TRUST.** The most direct route between point A and point B on your life-journey is the path of unwavering trust in Me. When your faith falters, you choose a trail that meanders and takes you well out of your way. You will get to point B eventually, but you will have lost precious time and energy. As soon as you realize you have wandered from your trust-path, look to Me and whisper, "I trust You, Jesus." This affirmation will help you get back on track.

The farther you roam along paths of unbelief, the harder it is to remember that I am with you. Anxious thoughts branch off in all directions, taking you farther and farther from awareness of My Presence. You need to voice your trust in Me frequently. This simple act of faith will keep you walking along straight paths with Me. *Trust in Me with all your heart, and I will make your paths straight.*

> *Trust in the LORD forever, for the LORD,*
> *the LORD, is the Rock eternal.*
>
> **ISAIAH 26:4**

*Also read:*

**PSALM 9:10; PSALM 25:4–5; PROVERBS 3:5–6**

# Worth the Risk

BE WILLING TO GO OUT ON A LIMB with Me. If that is where I am leading you, it is the safest place to be. Your desire to live a risk-free life is a form of unbelief. Your longing to live close to Me is at odds with your attempts to minimize risk. You are approaching a crossroads in your journey. In order to follow Me wholeheartedly, you must relinquish your tendency to play it safe.

Let Me lead you step by step through this day. If your primary focus is on Me, you can walk along perilous paths without being afraid. Eventually, you will learn to relax and enjoy the adventure of our journey together. As long as you stay close to Me, My sovereign Presence protects you wherever you go.

*Even though I walk through the valley of the shadow*
*of death, I will fear no evil, for you are with me;*
*your rod and your staff, they comfort me.*

**PSALM 23:4**

*Also read:*

**PSALM 9:10; JOHN 12:26**

# Accept My Time Frame

I AM WORKING ON YOUR BEHALF. Bring Me all your concerns, including your dreams. Talk with Me about everything, letting the Light of My Presence shine on your hopes and plans. Spend time allowing My Light to infuse your dreams with life, gradually transforming them into reality. This is a very practical way of collaborating with Me. I, the Creator of the universe, have deigned to cocreate with you. Do not try to hurry this process. If you want to work with Me, you have to accept My time frame. Hurry is not in My nature. Abraham and Sarah had to wait many years for the fulfillment of My promise, a son. How their long wait intensified their enjoyment of this child! *Faith is the assurance of things hoped for, perceiving as real fact what is not revealed to the senses.*

*For with you is the fountain of life; in your light we see light.*

PSALM 36:9

*Also read:*

GENESIS 21:1–7; HEBREWS 11:1 AMP

# With Every Fiber

**TRUST ME WITH EVERY FIBER** of your being! What I can accomplish in and through you is proportional to how much you depend on Me. One aspect of this is the degree to which you trust Me in a crisis or major decision. Some people fail miserably here, while others are at their best in tough times. Another aspect is even more telling: the constancy of your trust in Me. People who rely on Me in the midst of adversity may forget about Me when life is flowing smoothly. Difficult times can jolt you into awareness of your need for Me, whereas *smooth sailing* can lull you into the stupor of self-sufficiency.

I care as much about your tiny trust-steps through daily life as about your dramatic leaps of faith. You may think that no one notices, but the One who is always beside you sees everything— and rejoices. Consistently trusting in Me is vital to flourishing in My Presence.

> *Blessed is the man who makes the LORD his trust, who does not look to the proud, to those who turn aside to false gods.*
>
> **PSALM 40:4**

*Also read:*

**PSALM 56:3–4; PSALM 62:8; ISAIAH 26:3–4**

# Weakness

# Ever-Present Help

SOFTLY I ANNOUNCE MY PRESENCE. Shimmering hues of radiance tap gently at your consciousness, seeking entrance. Though I have all Power in heaven and on earth, I am infinitely tender with you. The weaker you are, the more gently I approach you. Let your weakness be a door to My Presence. Whenever you feel inadequate, remember that I am your *ever-present Help.*

Hope in Me, and you will be protected from depression and self-pity. Hope is like a golden cord connecting you to heaven. The more you cling to this cord, the more I bear the weight of your burdens; thus, you are lightened. Heaviness is not of My kingdom. Cling to hope, and My rays of Light will reach you through the darkness.

*God is our refuge and strength, an ever-present help in trouble.*

PSALM 46:1

*Also read:*

ROMANS 12:12; ROMANS 15:13

LET ME BLESS YOU with My grace and Peace. Open your heart and mind to receive all that I have for you. Do not be ashamed of your emptiness. Instead, view it as the optimal condition for being filled with My Peace.

It is easy to touch up your outward appearance, to look as if you have it all together. Your attempts to look good can fool most people. But I see straight through you, into the depths of your being. There is no place for pretense in your relationship with Me. Rejoice in the relief of being fully understood. Talk with Me about your struggles and feelings of inadequacy. Little by little, I will transform your weaknesses into strengths. Remember that your relationship with Me is saturated in grace. Therefore, *nothing that you do or don't do can separate you from My Presence.*

> *But the LORD said to Samuel, "Do not consider his appearance or his height, for I have rejected him. The LORD does not look at the things man looks at. Man looks at the outward appearance, but the LORD looks at the heart."*

1 SAMUEL 16:7

*Also read:*

ROMANS 8:38–39

# The Safest Place to Be

COME TO ME with all your weaknesses: physical, emotional, and spiritual. Rest in the comfort of My Presence, remembering that *nothing is impossible with Me.*

Pry your mind away from your problems so you can focus your attention on Me. Recall that I am *able to do immeasurably more than all you ask or imagine.* Instead of trying to direct Me to do this and that, seek to attune yourself to what I am *already* doing.

When anxiety attempts to wedge its way into your thoughts, remind yourself that *I am your Shepherd.* The bottom line is that I am taking care of you; therefore, you needn't be afraid of anything. Rather than trying to maintain control over your life, abandon yourself to My will. Though this may feel frightening—even dangerous—the safest place to be is in My will.

*For nothing is impossible with God.*

LUKE 1:37

*Also read:*

EPHESIANS 3:20–21; PSALM 23:1–4

IT IS GOOD THAT YOU RECOGNIZE your weakness. That keeps you looking to Me, your Strength. Abundant life is not necessarily health and wealth; it is living in continual dependence on Me. Instead of trying to fit this day into a preconceived mold, relax and be on the lookout for what I am doing. This mind-set will free you to enjoy Me and to find what I have planned for you to do. This is far better than trying to make things go according to your own plan.

Don't take yourself so seriously. Lighten up and laugh with Me. You have Me on your side, so what are you worried about? I can equip you to do absolutely anything, as long as it is My will. The more difficult your day, the more I yearn to help you. Anxiety wraps you up in yourself, trapping you in your own thoughts. When you look to Me and whisper My Name, you break free and receive My help. Focus on Me, and you will find Peace in My Presence.

*I have strength for all things in Christ Who empowers me [I am ready for anything and equal to anything through Him Who infuses inner strength into me; I am self-sufficient in Christ's sufficiency].*

PHILIPPIANS 4:13 AMP

*Also read:*

PROVERBS 17:22

# Blessed Through Weakness

COME TO ME when you are weak and weary. Rest snugly in My everlasting arms. I do not despise your weakness, My child. Actually, it draws Me closer to you because weakness stirs up My compassion—My yearning to help. Accept yourself in your weariness, knowing that I understand how difficult your journey has been.

Do not compare yourself with others who seem to skip along their life-paths with ease. Their journeys have been different from yours, and I have gifted them with abundant energy. I have gifted you with fragility, providing opportunities for your spirit to blossom in My Presence. Accept this gift as a sacred treasure: delicate, yet glowing with brilliant Light. Rather than struggling to disguise or deny your weakness, allow Me to bless you richly through it.

> *"A bruised reed he will not break, and a smoldering wick he will not snuff out. In faithfulness he will bring forth justice."*

**ISAIAH 42:3**

*Also read:*

**ISAIAH 54:10; ROMANS 8:26**

*YOUR NEEDS AND MY RICHES* are a perfect fit. I never meant for you to be self-sufficient. Instead, I designed you to need Me not only for daily bread but also for fulfillment of deep yearnings. I carefully crafted your longings and feelings of incompleteness to point you to Me. Therefore, do not try to bury or deny these feelings. Beware also of trying to pacify these longings with lesser gods: people, possessions, power.

Come to Me in all your neediness, with defenses down and with desire to be blessed. As you spend time in My Presence, your deepest longings are fulfilled. Rejoice in your neediness, which enables you to find intimate completion in Me.

*And my God will meet all your needs according
to his glorious riches in Christ Jesus.*

**PHILIPPIANS 4:19**

*Also read:*

**COLOSSIANS 2:2–3; PSALM 84:11–12 NKJV**

# Worth

# The Only Source of Affirmation

STOP JUDGING AND EVALUATING YOURSELF, for this is not your role. Above all, stop comparing yourself with other people. This produces feelings of pride or inferiority, sometimes a mixture of both. I lead each of My children along a path that is uniquely tailor-made for him or her. Comparing is not only wrong; it is also meaningless.

Don't look for affirmation in the wrong places: your own evaluations or those of other people. The only source of real affirmation is My unconditional Love. Many believers perceive Me as an unpleasable Judge, angrily searching out their faults and failures. Nothing could be farther from the truth! I died for your sins so that I might *clothe you in My garments of salvation*. This is how I see you: *radiant in My robe of righteousness*. When I discipline you, it is never in anger or disgust; it is to prepare you for face-to-Face fellowship with Me throughout all eternity. Immerse yourself in My loving Presence. Be receptive to My affirmation, which flows continually from the throne of grace.

> *"Do not judge, and you will not be judged. Do not condemn, and you will not be condemned. Forgive, and you will be forgiven."*
>
> LUKE 6:37

*Also read:*

ISAIAH 61:10 NASB; PROVERBS 3:11–12

# Measuring Up

I LOVE YOU REGARDLESS of how well you are performing. Sometimes you feel uneasy, wondering if you are doing enough to be worthy of My Love. No matter how exemplary your behavior, the answer to that question will always be no. Your performance and My Love are totally different issues, which you need to sort out. *I love you with an everlasting Love* that flows out from eternity without limits or conditions. *I have clothed you in My robe of righteousness*, and this is an eternal transaction: Nothing and no one can reverse it. Therefore, your accomplishment as a Christian has no bearing on My Love for you. Even your ability to assess how well you are doing on a given day is flawed. Your limited human perspective and the condition of your body, with its mercurial variations, distort your evaluations.

Bring your performance anxiety to Me, and receive in its place *My unfailing Love*. Try to stay conscious of My loving Presence with you in all that you do, and I will direct your steps.

> *The LORD appeared to us in the past, saying: "I have loved you with an everlasting love; I have drawn you with loving-kindness."*
>
> JEREMIAH 31:3

*Also read:*

ISAIAH 61:10; PSALM 31:16; PSALM 107:8

WHEN SOME BASIC NEED IS LACKING—time, energy, money—consider yourself blessed. Your very lack is an opportunity to latch on to Me in unashamed dependence. When you begin a day with inadequate resources, you must concentrate your efforts on the present moment. This is where you are meant to live—in the present. It is the place where I always await you. Awareness of your inadequacy is a rich blessing, training you to rely wholeheartedly on Me.

The truth is that self-sufficiency is a myth perpetuated by pride and temporary success. Health and wealth can disappear instantly, as can life itself. Rejoice in your insufficiency, knowing that *My Power is made perfect in weakness.*

> *Consider it pure joy, my brothers, whenever you*
> *face trials of many kinds, because you know that the*
> *testing of your faith develops perseverance.*
>
> JAMES 1:2–3

> *Also read:*
>
> 2 CORINTHIANS 12:9 NASB

# Worthy of Love

I WANT YOU TO EXPERIENCE the riches of your salvation: the Joy of being loved constantly and perfectly. You make a practice of judging yourself, based on how you look or behave or feel. If you like what you see in the mirror, you feel a bit more worthy of My Love. When things are going smoothly and your performance seems adequate, you find it easier to believe you are My beloved child. When you feel discouraged, you tend to look inward so you can correct whatever is wrong.

Instead of trying to "fix" yourself, *fix your gaze on Me, the Lover of your soul*. Rather than using your energy to judge yourself, redirect it to praising Me. Remember that I see you clothed in My righteousness, radiant in My perfect Love.

*In order that in the coming ages he might show the incomparable riches of his grace, expressed in his kindness to us in Christ Jesus. For it is by grace you have been saved, through faith— and this not from yourselves, it is the gift of God.*

EPHESIANS 2:7–8

*Also read:*

HEBREWS 3:1; PSALM 34:5

OPEN YOUR MIND AND HEART—your entire being—to receive My Love in full measure. So many of My children limp through their lives starved for Love because they haven't learned the art of receiving. This is essentially an act of faith: believing that I love you with boundless, everlasting Love. The art of receiving is also a discipline: training your mind to trust Me, coming close to Me with confidence.

Remember that the evil one is the *father of lies*. Learn to recognize his deceptive intrusions into your thoughts. One of his favorite deceptions is to undermine your confidence in My unconditional Love. Fight back against these lies! Do not let them go unchallenged. *Resist the devil in My Name, and he will slink away from you. Draw near to Me*, and My Presence will envelop you in Love.

*I pray that out of his glorious riches he may strengthen you with power through his Spirit in your inner being, so that Christ may dwell in your hearts through faith. And I pray that you, being rooted and established in love, may have power, together with all the saints, to grasp how wide and long and high and deep is the love of Christ.*

EPHESIANS 3:16–19

*Also read:*

HEBREWS 4:16; JOHN 8:44; JAMES 4:7–8 NKJV

# Wonderfully Made

I AM WITH YOU AND ALL AROUND YOU, encircling you in golden rays of Light. I always behold you Face-to-face. Not one of your thoughts escapes My notice. Because I am infinite, I am able to love you as if you and I were the only ones in the universe.

Walk with Me in intimate Love-steps, but do not lose sight of My Majesty. I desire to be your closest Friend, yet I am also your sovereign Lord. I created your brain with capacity to know Me as Friend and Lord simultaneously. The human mind is the pinnacle of My creation, but so few use it for its primary purpose—knowing Me. I communicate continually through My Spirit, My Word, and My creation. Only humans are capable of receiving Me and responding to My Presence. You are indeed *fearfully and wonderfully made*!

> *I sought the LORD, and he answered me; he delivered me from all my fears. Those who look to him are radiant; their faces are never covered with shame. This poor man called, and the LORD heard him; he saved him out of all his troubles.*

> PSALM 34:4–6

> *Also read:*

> 2 PETER 1:16–17; JOHN 17:3; PSALM 139:14

BEWARE OF SEEING YOURSELF through other people's eyes. There are several dangers to this practice. First of all, it is nearly impossible to discern what others actually think of you. Moreover, their views of you are variable: subject to each viewer's spiritual, emotional, and physical condition. The major problem with letting others define you is that it borders on idolatry. Your concern to please others dampens your desire to please Me, your Creator.

It is much more real to see yourself through *My eyes*. My gaze upon you is steady and sure, untainted by sin. Through My eyes you can see yourself as one who is deeply, eternally loved. Rest in My loving gaze, and you will receive deep Peace. Respond to My loving Presence by *worshiping Me in spirit and in truth*.

*And without faith it is impossible to please God, because anyone who comes to him must believe that he exists and that he rewards those who earnestly seek him.*

HEBREWS 11:6

*Also read:*

ROMANS 5:5; JOHN 4:23–24

SARAH YOUNG'S devotional writings are personal reflections from her daily quiet time of Bible reading, praying, and writing in prayer journals. With sales of more than 14 million books worldwide, *Jesus Calling*® has appeared on all major bestseller lists. Sarah's writings include *Jesus Calling*®, *Jesus Today*®, *Jesus Lives*™, *Dear Jesus*, *Jesus Calling*® *for Little Ones*, *Jesus Calling*® *Bible Storybook*, *Jesus Calling*®: *365 Devotions for Kids*, and *Peace in His Presence*—each encouraging readers in their journey toward intimacy with Christ. Sarah and her husband were missionaries in Japan and Australia for many years. They currently live in the United States.

*Jesus Calling*® was written to help people connect not only with Jesus, the living Word, but also with the Bible—the only infallible, inerrant Word of God. Sarah endeavors to keep her devotional writing consistent with that unchanging standard. Many readers have shared that Sarah's books have helped them grow to love God's Word. As Sarah states in the introduction to *Jesus Calling*®, "The devotions . . . are meant to be read slowly, preferably in a quiet place—with your Bible open."

Sarah is biblically conservative in her faith and reformed in her doctrine. She earned a master's degree in biblical studies and counseling from Covenant Theological Seminary in St. Louis. She is a member of the Presbyterian Church in America (PCA), where her husband, Stephen, is an ordained minister. Stephen and Sarah continue to be missionaries with Mission to the World, the PCA mission board.

Sarah spends a great deal of time in prayer, reading the Bible, and memorizing Scripture. She especially enjoys praying daily for readers of all her books.